FINTAN TALLON

GETTING
DOWN
TO
WORK

First published in 1993 by
Brandon Book Publishers Ltd,
Dingle, Co. Kerry

British Library Cataloguing in Publication Data is available for
this book.

ISBN 0 86322 169 6

Typeset by Brandon
Cover design by the Graphiconies, Dublin
Printed by Colour Books Ltds, Dublin

Acknowledgements

OVER THE PAST thirty years or more, I have trained under and worked with a vast number of dedicated professionals who have directed their talents and skills to the betterment of their fellow man. During that time I have shared their thoughts, absorbed their techniques of presenting ideas, and styled my own lectures and reports on the excellent example they set. To each and every one of these former colleagues and friends, I owe a deep depth of gratitude.

A very special acknowledgement is due to the late Ian Mikardo, economist and former chairman of the Labour Party. I remain indebted to him for my initial training and for being available to monitor and guide my work throughout the years. I am grateful for his encouragement for this work, and his, as always, constructive critical analysis.

A special word of thanks to Ciarán Piaras McCarthy for permitting me to read his thesis, "Social Change in Ireland 1961-91", which helped to guide my own research. To the people who shared with me the development of the Tallaght Programme, to each of the groups and the sponsoring Society, I owe the inspiration to write this book.

My gratitude also to my sister Maura, my daughter Miriam and my son Dara for their patience in proofreading my scripts and for their excellent suggestions all through. Finally, to my wife, Angela, and all of my family, who have sacrificed much in my pursuit of this dream, is owed a debt which can never be repaid. I dedicate this book to them.

Contents

The Crisis of Unemployment

TODAY I ATTENDED the funeral of a "failure". An overdose of barbiturates had caused his death.

Roger was a man in his early fifties. For more than twenty-five years of his life he had crafted jewellery, exquisite work which was prized by the young, the beautiful, the rich and the famous. Then, in the space of forty-eight hours, his world was shattered when his company went into liquidation. Roger's wife had died some years earlier and his children were scattered throughout the world; now years of industry had ended in failure. His craft was no longer in demand.

An inquest would later determine the cause of his death: unemployment would not feature in its report. It did, however, focus in the minds of the hundreds of friends, colleagues and former clients attending the funeral. Their lives had been enriched, however briefly, by a sensitive, compassionate man, a man of great charm and deep commitment to friendship.

Unemployment is not a set of statistics. It is a vast collection of human trauma, a social disease that wastes the energy, enthusiasm and skills of countless thousands. Above all it is a tragedy which denies to the nation the untapped potential of its people.

In June 1984, with the unemployment figures standing at 175,000, a small group of people held a public meeting in Dublin to launch a community self-help programme which became known as Success. As a guest speaker, I predicted that unemployment would continue to increase and would exceed 250,000 within three years unless deep-seated institutional change was brought about through genuine partnership between communities and government. A senior official spokesman disagreed; he predicted that planned government action would halve the unemployment figure over the next three years. Today the number of people out of work is rising beyond the 300,000 mark, and many observers believe that the official figures are understated.

Recent political events in Ireland and elsewhere have focused attention on this alarming growth in unemployment. In Ireland a new government took office in 1993 with a solemn promise to put unemployment at the top of its agenda. Pressure groups of all kinds demanded that the government act, amongst them the Irish bishops who published a pastoral on the social consequences of unemployment and in the west of the country formed a task force to influence government policy. In Britain, the two main parties fought the 1992 election on the basis of their ability to provide solutions to the unemployment crisis; ironically, upwards of a million British people were disenfranchised from voting because they were homeless, or had not paid a "poll tax".

But this party political approach to the problem is wrong. Governments do not create jobs, except the politicians' own and those in the public service needed to support the government structure. The state agencies, set up to achieve specific functions such as industrial promotion, training and export marketing, and to implement national policy in the field of commercial development, are not job-creation agencies; at best, their efforts can only facilitate others to generate new jobs. Neither is unemployment an illness that can be cured by simply injecting greater financial resources into the economy. The problem is much bigger and affects the entire social, economic and political system. It is not temporary: unemployment has been endemic in Ireland for over two centuries. It is not just caused by recession: that only makes matters worse. Clearly it is not confined to Ireland or other less developed countries: most industrial societies are experiencing the same problem, even if not to the same degree.

We are deluding ourselves if we think that a change of policies on interest rates, taxation or import controls can make a major difference on its own. These factors are important since each, *inter alia*, affects the climate for investment, employment, consumer demand and price competitiveness. However, our membership of the European Community and the European Monetary System (EMS), together with our acceptance of the disciplines of the Maastricht Treaty, severely limits our ability to operate such policies effectively. When Ireland joined the European Community, it required a separate protocol to allow it to continue using tax incentives to promote foreign investment in Ireland. This policy has been a mainstay of Irish economic development since the late 1950s, but must now be phased out, and will largely disappear by 1996. In the area of import controls, the European Court has already declared illegal our import duties against Northern Ireland and the UK.

Most forms of Keynesian economics are considered incompatible with free competition in an interdependent Europe. Of course, we cannot exclude macroeconomic policies in our search for solutions to unemployment. It would be a nonsense to argue that microeconomic solutions alone can solve our unemployment problem, and in any case there is a wide range of measures which the state can take to help create the climate for job creation and growth. But, if anything, an over-dependence on macroeconomic policies to the exclusion of microeconomic techniques has led to a great deal of our present difficulties.

Our most fundamental problem is that, for nearly half a century, politicians have been presenting themselves as the "Grand Providers", selling a vision of the caring state cosseting its people from the cradle to the grave. There is, however, a gap between the reality and the political rhetoric. Quite apart from the fact that the state cannot spend more than it obtains in either taxes or borrowing or – in the EC context – grants, state paternalism on a grand scale cannot be implemented without corrupting the individual quality of life and liberty. The ultimate horror of the puritan work ethic was that it made work sacred and money the key to a new heaven, but work and money are means to an end, which differs from person to person. Human beings have individual dreams and aspirations. Once the state takes control of our lives we are no longer free, but merely compliant people in a society ruled by bureaucrats where our freedom of expression and movement is ordered by writ and regulation.

For a time politicians can maintain the illusion of being the grand providers by borrowing improvidently, but eventually they are forced into structural adjustments to pay government debts. Then they claim that a prosperous future demands short-term pain; but when the promised utopia is not delivered, and without a true partnership between government and people it never can be, they turn to placebos. Thus we get large-scale training programmes producing people trained for non-existent jobs, an educational system bursting at the seams, and a social crisis reflected in our overflowing prisons and high rates of homelessness, drug abuse and violence.

I believe we can do better than this. After more than thirty years of working and lecturing on community enterprise initiatives and promoting the concept of genuine empowerment and partnership, I believe the present jobs crisis brings an opportunity to create for ourselves a more rewarding and caring lifestyle. The depth of the crisis forces us to open our minds, to consider ways in which we can construct a new path to a better future and build an economic order rooted in our local communities, one which brings stability and fulfilment to our working lives. Can it be done? The evidence that it can is to be seen in a host of local initiatives which have sprung up throughout the western world. Indeed, all the evidence points to the fact that the unemployment crisis cannot be solved without sustained community action. Philip Mullally, chief executive of the enterprise trust set up under the Programme for Economic and Social Partnership, warns that "The administration of the promised EC billions in Ireland could unintentionally reinforce the dependency culture and put local employment initiatives at risk," and goes on: "Local people must set the agenda for job creation. Only in this way can creative energies be released to revitalise the economic life of communities."

When we look at unemployment on a national or global scale, the problem seems too vast, almost remote from our lives. We recognise that the situation is intolerable, but become numbed by the recital of facts and statistics which we cannot hope to grasp, much less control. But if we reduce these numbers to local level we scale the problem down to human size: the unemployed are now our husbands, wives, brothers, sisters, neighbours and friends. We begin to face the reality that, even if we have a job, the cancer of unemployment spreads its effects through every living fibre of society. Now we are forced to avoid the escapist route of asking what *they* are doing to solve the problem – *they* being the government, the banks, the churches or any other impersonal institution – and instead, if we are honest, we seek to find out what we can do, as individuals and as a community.

This book sets out to explore answers to that question. To do so we need to understand our past as well as our present, to know where we are coming from as well as where we are going. In presenting my analysis of the community enterprise approach, I will concentrate largely on job-creation initiatives that can be achieved by local individuals and communities. Local initiative can make an enormous contribution to creating employment, and can be the catalyst for further change at regional and national level. Broader change is needed: community initiative on its own cannot eliminate unemployment without substantial matching action by government and its agencies. We outline the concept of the modern enterprise community and the critical steps which must be taken by government in support of community action. This kind of support has been put in place elsewhere, and we look at its impact in the United Kingdom and the USA.

The approach to job creation set out in this book is not the only approach to tackling the unemployment crisis, nor does it discount the value of other measures which can be taken to alleviate the situation. But by starting at community level, with people, the community enterprise approach is the one which applies most directly to you and me.

Lessons of the Past

THE IRISH NATION was born with a legacy of unemployment. In 1919, three years before independence, the founders of the emerging nation published a democratic programme which declared: "It is the duty of the nation to ensure every citizen ... the opportunity to spend his or her strength in the service of the nation." In return for the people's service they guaranteed, in the name of the republic, "the right of every citizen to an adequate share of the produce of the nation's labour".

Their concern was well founded. For centuries, under British rule, Ireland had been the poor relation of its neighbour. Its role was to export agricultural products to Britain and import British manufactures. Such industry as existed was closely linked to the needs of an agricultural economy, and though there was some substantial industry, largely in brewing and distilling, this also depended on processing and selling the produce of the farmer. Ireland had very few industries to match those of Britain – in a small and relatively impoverished country, industries catering primarily for consumers were not likely to grow large – and Irish manufacturing was in any case mainly controlled by British-owned subsidiaries.

However, there was a very considerable number of workshops supplying both manufacturing and services. Human needs were met by these local workshop industries or, in more remote areas, by itinerant craftsmen, and in the towns and villages barter was not uncommon. The local forge made gates and railings and built the frames for farm transport; the local shoemaker made and repaired shoes; carpentry workshops made and upholstered furniture – much of which is now valued as antiques – and there were a great many small workshops making and repairing household implements, very often from their own moulds. Much of this craft laid the basis for later small industries.

Through the last decades of the nineteenth century and the early years of the twentieth, employment opportunities in Ireland were limited. In the countryside peasant proprietors worked their own smallholdings and the itinerant farm labourer was hired by the day. Since the Famine, several thousand itinerant craftsmen did regular rounds of the towns, villages and farms. For those without their own homes life was particularly hard, and there was substantial migration into the cities in search of work. The cities had small clothing factories, foundries, print shops, but no adequate industrial base. As a colony Ireland exported its raw materials to feed factories and processing plants in the UK; cattle, for example, were exported on the hoof, and there was little encouragement to develop native processing of hides and skins. Scarce jobs were largely to be found in skilled and semi-skilled trades such as cabinet-making, leather-craft, tailoring, hairdressing and in the building sector. Road, rail and general transport absorbed some of the unskilled labour pool, but demand for work always exceeded the supply of jobs available. This led to substantial unemployment or under-employment, and of course to wholesale emigration. Yet, in the political struggle of the nineteenth century, politicians and revolutionaries alike ignored the extreme plight of the farm labourers in the countryside and the slum dwellers in the towns while they pursued other priorities.

In the first decade of this century the bulk of the working population in Dublin, numbering about 87,000, lived in slums. In the decaying inner city over 2,000 families were housed in single rooms without heat or light, usually sharing inadequate water supplies and sanitation. There were high rates of malnutrition, disease and death. Of the estimated 40,000 men in the labour force in Dublin in 1901, less than 15,000 had regular work in the skilled trades or transport. The majority found casual work when and where they could.

We need perhaps to be reminded that a previous generation, which helped to forge the nation's independence, overcame odds which were far greater than those we face today. Their action and sacrifice offer an example which can help to counteract the despair which pervades contemporary society. To a great extent that generation had a deep-rooted assurance of the natural order of life and a belief in a caring deity, a faith which sustained them in difficult times. They were imbued with a sense of duty, of obligation towards their neighbour, and a courage impervious to penury.

With the advent of independence in 1921, economic progress was slow and showed no appreciable growth through the decade. By 1930 Ireland still relied predominantly on agriculture although a policy of protectionism had helped to establish about 100 new factories employing some 13,000 people, very many of which were established with low-interest government loans. The first government of the Irish Free State was committed to an economic philosophy which regarded agriculture as the principal, if not the sole, source of the country's wealth, and saw Ireland's relationship with Britain, its main trading partner, as fundamental to Irish development. In his excellent review of this period in *Ireland Since the Famine*, Professor F.S.L. Lyons points out that the new state faced the harsh reality that political independence did not equate with economic independence. The pattern established in the latter part of the nineteenth century proved hard to break: the Irish Free State remained part of an economic complex in which the UK was the predominant partner. The Irish currency was still linked to sterling, 90% of Irish exports still looked to Britain or Northern Ireland for markets, and the Cosgrave government, like the former British one, still saw agriculture as the foundation of the country's wealth. Hoping that agricultural prosperity would lead in time to a modest expansion of home industry, the government had an intense fear that tariffs would provoke foreign retaliation. A few old tariffs, mainly on tobacco and cars, were continued with, later tariffs were added to articles such as boots, shoes, glass bottles, soaps, candles, clothing and confectionary. Generally, however, the attitude of the government was one of extreme caution towards the whole concept of industrial protection. Kevin O'Higgins, Minister for Home Affairs and then Justice, dismissed Arthur Griffith's recipe for developing native industry behind high tariff walls as little more than "propagandist writings".

Yet in a world of rising tariffs, Arthur Griffith's Sinn Féin doctrine of economic nationalism seemed increasingly relevant. Sinn Féin's successors, Fianna Fáil, were committed to a philosophy of political and economic independence. In 1928 a frustrated opposition spokesman named Sean Lemass, who would later become Minister for Industry and Commerce in the first Fianna Fáil government and, ultimately, de Valera's chosen successor, pleaded for greater use of tariff protection to support native industry, contending "Ireland can be made a self-contained unit, providing all of the necessities of living in adequate quantities for the people residing in this island at the moment, and probably for a much larger unit."

The impeccable orthodoxy which the Cosgrave government exercised in financial matters left little room in its budgets for public spending to upgrade the lives of the people. It is difficult to say with any precise accuracy the numbers unemployed in the new Irish state during the first decade or more after independence; the statistics for this period are both incomplete and suspect. However, to avoid starvation, people had either to find work, to emigrate or to receive assistance under the Poor Law Acts, the only form of social welfare then available. The population of the Irish Free State was estimated at 2.9 million in 1926. Over the next ten years, approximately 167,000 emigrated, while assistance under the Poor Laws was given to 48,000 in 1926, a figure which had grown to 77,000 by 1931. Then, in the 1930s, the political and economic situation worsened considerably.

The Cosgrave government of the 1920s had agreed with the

British government a series of financial payments arising out of the Treaty settlement. In summary these were: the collection and remittance of moneys from tenant purchasers arising from the compulsory acquisition of land from previous landlords; the payment of a contribution towards interest on Land Stock previously issued by the British government; the payment of a substantial proportion of the moneys required to fund pensions for former public servants; and, finally, the payment of £250,000 for sixty years to re-imburse the British for malicious damage claims arising from the War of Independence. The Cosgrave government took the view that these measures were a valid follow-up to the Treaty commitments; accordingly, these "agreements" were never brought before the Dáil for ratification and were not actually published until 1932. When de Valera's party took office after the 1932 general election, it rejected Britain's right to these payments. It argued that, in default of Dáil ratification, these so-called "agreements" were not binding. In addition, the new government introduced an extensive range of tariffs to protect Irish industry.

The British government's response was swift and extensive. It imposed tariffs on Irish agricultural imports, withdrew from Ireland all entitlement to Commonwealth preferential tariffs, imposed stringent quotas on the import of Irish fat cattle and banned the import of Irish store cattle, beef and veal. Ireland answered by establishing penal tariffs on all British imports including coal, coke, cement, electrical goods, machinery, iron and steel. Since Britain was Ireland's largest customer, this economic war gravely affected agricultural earnings and severely impaired Ireland's overall economic plans; in a world already deep in depression, Ireland had no alternative markets. The farming community's income was drastically reduced and this, in turn, diminished the demand for other Irish-produced goods.

The "hungry thirties" were aptly named. Ireland survived, largely thanks to the very substantial remittances received from Irish emigrants living and working abroad. The economic war also posed a grave threat to the country's political stability. William T. Cosgrave, while opposing the de Valera measures democratically, showed great courage in refusing to bend to his party's more militant "blueshirt" wing which threatened a revival of civil-war politics. Indeed, it is a tribute to the leadership qualities of all of the main political parties, and to the maturity of our people, that a descent into anarchy was avoided.

Despite the undoubted hardship created by the economic war, the Fianna Fáil government relentlessly pursued its policies of economic nationalism. Amongst other things, it made a serious and prolonged attempt to redress the balance between different sectors of the economy. The government tried to free the countryside from the dominance of the cattleman by extending the area under tillage, and it worked to develop home industries. However, as the then Banking Commission observed: "An industrial programme has hardly had a fair chance to succeed at a time when a large section of the market for industrial goods is severely curtailed."

The trade war was finally settled in 1938. The Irish government agreed to make a payment of £10 million to Britain in settlement of all claims and subsequently the pre-1932 trade position and concessions were fully restored by both countries. However, within a year of the economic war ending, a far greater conflict had erupted over Europe.

Throughout the Emergency, as the Second World War was called in Ireland, the country's young industries, more than half of which had been established only in the previous decade, could not provide enough jobs to counter unemployment. Nett emigration in the ten years 1936-46 was 187,000, and when post-war re-construction brought virtual full employment to Britain, the high wages which followed attracted further emigration from Ireland; from 1947 to 1951 some 119,000 people left the country. The traffic across the Irish Sea also raised illusory hopes of an equality of living standards in the two countries, which forced the Irish government into a decade of heavy state borrowing, largely directed into social welfare. Politicians desperately strove to walk the tightrope between high expectations and affordable objectives, between providing work and reducing emigration while simultaneously giving higher levels of amenities and services. Borrowing which had started in the 1950s developed a self-sustaining cycle as "auction politics" took hold and politicians began more and more to promote a doctrine which cast the state in the role of grand provider.

In 1958 Dr T.K. Whitaker, Secretary of the Department of Finance, introduced his first report on economic development.

After thirty-five years of native government people are asking whether we can achieve an acceptable degree of economic progress. The common talk amongst parents, in the towns as in rural Ireland, is of their children having to emigrate as soon as their education is complete to be sure of a reasonable livelihood.

Bowing to the weight of these circumstances, Ireland embarked on a sea-change in economic policy. The Industrial Development (Encouragement of External Investment) Act 1958 withdrew Ireland's tariff barriers and import quotas, and outlined a set of tax and other concessions to foreign industry in order to attract investment into the country. In effect, Ireland had set about changing from a closed, self-sufficient society to an open economy.

The First Programme for Economic Expansion concentrated principally on expanding the agricultural economy, targeting beef production in particular; it planned to upgrade grassland, eradicate bovine TB, market Irish meat more effectively and educate farmers in modern methods of farming. A "vast increase in private industrial investment" was to be achieved by enticing foreign capital with tax concessions, subventing the cost of machinery, providing technical assistance and other benefits. Foreign industries were offered grants of up to 50% of capital costs subject to 90% export of product, and total tax exemption on profits and dividends for ten years, with graded exemption for the succeeding five years. Protection for protection's sake was to be eliminated. There was a basic assumption that future participation in some form of European Economic Community made the old aim of self-sufficiency unrealistic.

The new policy was sold to the public as a remedy for all ills: in particular, it promised to deliver the dream of full employment and enable any emigrant who wanted to return to do so. Of course, Whitaker was far too cautious a man to be directly responsible for this oversell. However, as the most senior civil servant involved in preparing the First Programme, it is surprising that he did not anticipate what the politicians would do with his already up-beat estimations of the programme's likely outcome. Politicians, for their part, felt they needed to put forward the strongest possible case for the new policy, and stressed its positive benefits. This optimism was felt to be all the more necessary when the programme would require an increase in state subvention of the order of £53 million plus for the five years of the plan.

There were other subjective attitudes helping to push the country on this new path. By the time the First Programme for Economic Expansion was being considered, Irish industry and services had come to be regarded as overprotected and inefficient, a burden on the economy. The acceptance of this highly political and subjective viewpoint, together with a lack of basic research into or adequate consultation with Irish industry, made Whitaker's general indictment of past policies somewhat suspect. The evidence, for example, that in 1957 manufacturing industries' exports had increased by 30% to £17 million was available, but ignored.

The First Programme was estimated to cost £53.4 million for the term of the plan, but when this was added to the cost of existing schemes, spending on economic expansion came to a formidable total of £220.4 million over five years. Nonetheless, the programme was generally hailed as a success; even today it is regarded as having promoted a major advance in Irish economic development. The level of success in the agricultural industry may have been limited, as a result of bad planning and an over-emphasis on beef production, but on the other hand industrial output rose by 47% between 1957 and 1963. In a review of the programme Dr Whitaker remarked: "The success of the programme is represented above all by a pronounced change in national mentality."

A Second Programme was introduced in 1963 to cover the period up to 1970. It confidently anticipated exports of goods and services to rise by 75% in ten years, nett employment to rise by 81,000 and nett emigration to fall to 10,000 per annum. This leap in the dark projection was confounded within a year, when Britain, then in economic crisis, slammed a 15% levy on all imports. In the following year, 1965, the Anglo-Irish Trade Agreement set the basis for a free trade area between both countries, but by now the combined effect of the premature dismantling of protection for Irish industry and the new agreement to phase out special terms to foreign investors and management, made the prospect of achieving the programmes targets very unlikely.

Nonetheless the 1960s was a time of vibrant social and political change. There was a general belief that the boom years were coming (or – whisper it – were here), and a *laissez faire* economic philosophy dominated political thinking. "A rising tide raises all boats" was the catchphrase, and there were substantial improvements in social welfare, with "free education" being introduced for the first time by the state. The very fact that emigrants were coming home broke an important economic and psychological barrier. The population increased by about 100,000 between 1962 and 1971, and grew by a further 500,000 in the following ten years. There was a significant shift in types of employment; people moved out of agriculture into factories and service industries, and moved from the countryside to the city. The first stirrings of feminism gave rise, after a long struggle, to the much delayed implementation of equality legislation. Expanded educational opportunities and the bouyancy of the labour market generated high expectations for the future.

Yet these "boom years" yielded relatively little nett increase in employment. Very many of the jobs predicted when grants were being announced did not materialise and job creation only marginally exceeded job losses in any case. People were getting better-paid jobs and there was more spending money in circulation, a great deal of which had trickled through from foreign investment. But far too much government financial policy was based on expectations which were yet to be realised.

Whitaker, in drafting the First Programme for Economic Expansion, had been very flexible, reluctant to set specific targets to measure the programme's impact. He recognised that Ireland was exposed to many external pressures, some foreseeable, others less easy to predict. He was, however, convinced that Ireland's economic nationalism could not survive the postwar growth of free trade and the anticipated development of the EEC, and he believed it was a time when risks had to be taken. The Second Programme was more specific in terms of targets. Whether this was wise or not is a matter for judgement: Ireland was still exposed, as was demonstrated in 1965, to the same external pressures which had prompted Whitaker's earlier caution.

Pressure also came from within: the explosion of the Northern Ireland crisis had a profound effect on investment in the Republic. I am personally aware of five major developments that were cancelled because of the images of war in Ireland; I even had a call from one German client offering to take my wife and family out of danger. The 1970 Arms Trial crisis caused the abrupt cancellation of work being done in the planning of an £8 million foreign investment in the south-west.

The Programmes for Economic Expansion were to lay the foundations for our entry into the European Economic Community, which we joined in 1972. The strategic thinking on which the programmes were founded also motivated the setting up and subsequent expansion of a plethora of state agencies. National strategic programmes had brought the process of political decision-making into the arena of rational economic planning, and the soundness of the programmes' economic forecasts suffered as a result. The Second Programme for Economic Expansion anticipated growth targets which many economists and politicians felt were unreal. This flawed optimism gave an over-confident view of the nation's ability to survive the impact of EEC membership. There were solid grounds for doubting our readiness to assume the obligations of membership in the industrial area, and our agriculture had far too narrow a base both at the time of entry and since. A greater sense of realism might have provided grounds for negotiating a period of associate membership before assuming our full obligations in the Community. And, to a very large extent, as a people we were far too ready to replace one "big brother" with what we perceived as another with larger resources. For most of us, however, these doubts were all in the future. For now, the picture of our nation achieving European standards of wealth and comfort had an appeal which could not be denied.

The Era of the Economic Guru

I F THE FIRST forty years of independence were marked by a style of political decision making in which politicians took it on themselves to reveal the people's needs, the next thirty years elevated economists to the role of arbiters of economic policy. Perhaps our politicians might have adopted the gospel of Morris West's fictional creation, Cassidy:

Never debate political theory, that's an exercise in futility. Stay clear of professional economists: they can lose you an election, and still have tenure in their universities.

How well do economists face the challenge of a people growing up in a world without hope or opportunity? How, for example, do World Bank economists justify the imposition of policies which are designed more to protect western banks than to serve the needs of people who have only recently achieved freedom? In Britain, where the proportion of people employed in manufacturing industry is rapidly declining, of what comfort is former Chancellor Nigel Lawson's comment that "Most of the jobs of the future will be in service industries, not high-tech or low-tech but no-tech"? As Professor Abba Lerner of Roosevelt College said in a lecture published in 1953, "Economic theory, like other fields of activity, suffers from an unprecedented rate of obsolescence."

It would be foolish to argue that economists have no useful role or that plans for economic development are unnecessary. However, I do submit that Irish economic policies, the way in which they have been implemented, and in particular the way in which they have encouraged an expectation that a prosperous future can be achieved in a relatively short time, have all contributed to the sense of powerlessness which has overtaken us now that we are faced with the depths of the jobs crisis.

The foremost economic planner Ireland has produced and the architect of our first economic programme, T.K. Whitaker, can himself be faulted. Whitaker, and the politicians he served, adopted too readily the consensus view that our principal national strength lay in agriculture and that we lacked the ability and skills to develop worthwhile native industry. Manufacturing industry was seen as being geared to the small, protected home market; as a result Ireland's economic plans adopted the view that any significant industrial development would depend on the enterprise of foreign entrepreneurs. Having adopted this negative thinking, economists and politicians made little effort to plan the development of existing Irish industries. Little effective research was done to explore their work, their potential for growth, or the vital role they played in the social fabric of our communities, and although various industrial committees were set up to assist Irish industry adapt to free trade conditions, they were made toothless by inadequate funding. In effect, Irish industry was officially regarded as a lost cause.

The national programmes for economic expansion poured considerable resources into developing an industrial economy by attracting foreign industries. This policy was justified on the basis that it helped to build Ireland's industrial base and reduce the country's over-dependence on agriculture. However, while this open investment policy had its positive aspects, it also had its downside. It led, for example, to the major part of our distribution and retail sector being acquired by foreign investors, and the subsequent growth in the supermarket culture, which bought very much of its product from abroad, eventually diminished our native production of food. Ireland had for many years produced the bulk of its own food needs and, particularly during the war years, exported substantial quantities to the UK; over time that situation was reversed and nowadays our food imports are alarmingly high. Basic consumer goods which could be produced in Ireland – fruit, vegetables, leather goods, shoes and clothing – feature heavily in our import statistics.

As traditional native industries closed down, jobs were lost, principally in rural areas. At the same time as Irish industry declined, the numbers staying at work or seeking employment grew dramatically, because of the implementation of equality legislation which enabled upwards of 65,000 married women to stay in work after marriage, the "baby boom" of the 1960s and '70s, and the return of emigrants with their families. There was massive migration once more to the cities or abroad, and the heart was torn out of many of our towns and villages. Some readers will remember the late John Healy, in a memorable series of articles in *The Irish Times*, desperately pleading for somebody to call "Stop".

Economic planners failed to recognise that Irish industries were operated and controlled by people with strong local roots who had, in general, made a commitment to their area. The motives of the foreign investor were far more self-interested. In many cases they established no more than assembly operations to facilitate international mobility of funds so as to avoid paying tax. Some were attracted by grants and tax concessions, and came to Ireland at the expense of other locations and workers who had served their useful life as far as corporate policy was concerned.

The Industrial Development Authority (IDA), set up to promote economic development, grew instead as a marketing agency and failed to take on a fully fledged developmental role. Its officers, perhaps understandably, preferred the excitement and career opportunities which contact with foreign industry entailed, to the more humdrum task of nursing the native entrepreneur. An elitism came to be attached to working with big, foreign industries; this attitude traversed the whole spectrum, from the job preferences of the professionals, through the attitudes of politicians and public servants, to acceptability for loans by financial institutions.

As the value of foreign enterprise grew to dominate economic thought, pride in being Irish was rapidly eroded. Respect for goods made in Ireland became diminished. The ac-

quisition by foreign investors of the largest segment of our distribution industry and the dramatic growth in the supermarket culture caused little public outcry; yet, overall, the new owners showed scant regard for Irish economic development, pursuing policies of "profit-dominated" importing of goods. When this policy played a primary role in forcing the closure of one native company after another, their apparent failure simply worked to justify the contemptuous attitude held towards Irish-based industry. The fact that many survived, despite the odds, owes more to the combined determination of owners and workers alike than to any pro-active encouragement offered either by the state or its economic policies.

The absence of an effective development agency might have been offset if, following the programmes for economic expansion, the Department of Finance had developed an entrepreneurial role rather than acting merely as the country's bookkeeper. Instead, budgetary procedures became primarily a problem of attempting to balance the books. Too often this was done in ways which were to affect employment negatively. Examples abound: for instance, placing such a high local rates burden on industry and business, or raising direct and indirect taxes without making any real effort to determine their effect on employment. The majority of native businesses were forced into the costly role of tax collectors through the regulations governing VAT and PRSI. Most Irish industries paid VAT on purchases with specific rights to claim in arrears for goods exported, whereas foreign industry obtained VAT exemption as exporters and in general, having received capital grants and committments to tax exemptions, had far less overhead costs in accounting, bridging finance, and so on. So day by day, in town and countryside, small businesses which had previously provided tax-generating income were collapsing, very often by Revenue writ.

Multinationals now account for about 50% of manufacturing employment in Ireland, providing 87,000 direct and some 90,000 indirect jobs. In the main they import raw materials

and export profits and management fees. Their exports foster the illusion of healthy trade balances, constantly quoted as a barometer of the nation's economic health. Since the mid-'70s four high-tech industries – electronic, computer, instrument engineering, and pharmaceutical firms – have accounted for nearly half of Ireland's industrial output, but barely employ one-fifth of its manufacturing workforce. It is fair to ask, as Dr FitzGerald does, "whether perhaps there might not have been some other way in which part at least of the hundreds of millions of pounds of industrial grants paid to these 150 or so firms could have been deployed differently, so as to provide more than the relatively small figure of about 15,000 additional jobs that have been created in these four sectors."[1]

To an extent, the basic theory of this economic policy seem to have grown from a feeling of inferiority rather than from sound economic thinking. The lack of any stringent assessment of the value of such development became very evident in the mid-'80s when a "black hole", as it was called, was discovered in the Irish economy. Through this hole some £800m. flowed out of the Irish economy annually in repatriated profits.[2] Its discovery generated much alarm amongst economists and others, but one wonders why it should have done; after all, multinational companies had come to Ireland to create profits for their shareholders, and had legally binding commitments from the state which allowed them to send these profits abroad, without being subject to the normal exchange controls. A further source of surprise to many agencies engaged in fostering multinational-led development was the degree to which these industries failed to establish linkages with Irish firms. Again, the theory that multinational industry would lift the overall level of economic activity by drawing on Irish companies for components and services proved incorrect. Some did, when it was economic and profitable to do so, but the majority already had established sources of supply which, because of their scale, could produce more competitively than Irish suppliers.

The fragile nature of this industrial base, the future of which will always depend on the impersonal decision making of foreign boards of management, has become all too apparent. Multinational employment is important, but we have developed an unhealthy overdependency on such industry. When multinational plants are threatened, our politicians and industrial agencies engage in a flurry of activity to try to avert closure and make good the damage which it will cause. One wonders if the break-up of our leather, chipboard, paper, clothing, milling and other industries could have been avoided by a similar display of concern.

Let me give an example of one such closure which could have been avoided. As nominee of a major shareholder, with the support of the management of Munster Chipboard, I sought from the Irish government free access to our state forestry thinning: this was the arrangement enjoyed by our Scandinavian competitors in their home countries. In Ireland, however, manufacturers were forced to tender for this wood, creating a raw material cost of upwards of £20 per ton. The shareholders were prepared to make a further substantial investment in the company provided it received the same privileges as were given by other governments to their industries.

The Irish government refused to agree these conditions, a decision which caused the collapse of the chipboard industry and probably contributed to the termination of Clondalkin Paper Mills' main operation. With the closure of these industries, Irish forestry thinnings were exported to Scandinavia at a price of £1 per ton out of Waterford port, a price which did not even cover the cost to the state of felling and transport. The burden of social welfare to the hundreds of redundant workers was also assumed by the state. Today, the decaying shells of these factories stand as a monument to the poor judgement of our political leaders. It is now proposed to revive this industry in a joint venture between the semi-state sector and multinational industry, but at best this move is only recovering ground lost in the past twenty years. In France, Germany, the Benelux countries and elsewhere, governments realise they have a responsibility to native industry. A senior European Commission official commented privately: "The British opt out of the social charter. The French, Germans, Belgians, Dutch and Spanish use dubious pro-active, positive discrimination in favour of their native product to enhance market protection. But the Irish, like good Christians, abide by all of the EC commandments, losing jobs and markets to their competitors."

Dr Whitaker had applied to the Irish situation economic doctrines which had been current in other countries, and the economists who followed in his footsteps maintained the practice. But "the past," as Harold Macmillan was fond of quoting, "is a foreign country. They do things differently there." Historians may learn much from the past, if only because history has a habit of repeating itself, but for economists the age-old problem of how best to manage resources must always face new circumstances and new situations. There is a thread-worn story, told often in economist circles, about the new economics professor who was pondering what questions to set in his first exam paper. An older colleague handed him the previous year's paper and advised him dryly, "We always use the same questions; we merely change the answers."

Economics is not an exact science. Economic analysis is important to decision making, but it is only one element in a complex social equation. Any successful manager realises this and, while weighing the advice given, decides ultimately on the basis of his or her own assessment of all the relevant factors, including the management of human resources, long-term strategic goals, and so on. If the country as a whole had the benefit of good executive leadership, mistakes, many of which were due to a shortsighted approach to problem solving, could have been avoided. Unfortunately, our very structures of government deny access to men and women of the calibre we need. Another very basic factor in degrading the quality of economic perception is the growing practice of television analysis, which demands instant answers to every question. The viewer expects the guru to know. Many economists will admit to being embarrassed by the responses they have given in the high pressure arena of the television studio, and recognise, on calmer reflection, that their prognosis should be qualified, dealt with more comprehensively, or even retracted.

The debate on Ireland's entry into the EEC is a case in point. Economists and opinion makers lined up to confront the issue and, indeed, the public. Those who favoured joining argued that we needed to replace the British cheap food policy with the European guaranteed price system in order to ensure income stability for farmers, and suggested that if we remained outside the Community Irish agriculture would go into a decline which would drag the country back to the hungry '30s. Whitaker's analysis, it was argued, showed that Ireland could profitably assume full membership; more than that, an integrated Europe would upgrade the economies of the poorer regions, and Ireland would benefit substantially as a result. It was held that emigration to Britain would almost certainly be curtailed if Britain were to join the Community while Ireland remained outside, while, if we did join, our people could get jobs all over Europe. It was argued consistantly that employment depended on attracting foreign industry, and if Ireland failed to join the EEC foreign industry would desert our shores.

Those opposing membership argued that Irish agriculture was too underdeveloped to take full advantage of the European programme. As regards employment they pointed out that Irish employment consisted of both native and foreign industry and that native industry, including the labour-intensive assembly sector, would be decimated in the EEC. They argued that if Europe was as altruistic as those proposing membership suggested, surely it would recognise Ireland's level of relative underdevelopment and allow it negotiate a long period of associate membership to enable Ireland to adapt to these new economic conditions. At the same time they argued that nationalism would always pervade European economic practice, and that foreign industry too would eventually desert Ireland and site nearer the centre of mainland

Europe. It was pointed out, too, that if the UK did join she would constantly opt out if she did not get her own way.

We can measure the accuracy of all these statements more objectively with the benefit of hindsight. At the time, though, the differing prognosis given for Ireland's fortunes were revealing and misleading in almost equal measure. Each diagnosis highlighted one aspect of the problem; what was required was a capacity for management which could take the best advice available and use it to direct the country on the course which best suited its talents and goals. This capacity was, however, profoundly absent.

Through the 1970s and '80s the profession of economic guru became a growth industry in itself. No self-respecting political party or industry, bank, employer organisation or trade union could claim credibility without having on hand its own economist, either in-house or on retainer. Economist Martin O'Donoghue, credited with authorship of the programme which led to Fianna Fáil's famous victory in 1977, was appointed a senior minister in the newly created Economics Department of the subsequent government. Fine Gael went one better, appointing economist Garret FitzGerald as party leader in 1977; when he formed the Coalition government of 1981 he appointed another economist, Alan Dukes, first to the industry ministry and then to finance. Mr Dukes later succeeded Dr FitzGerald as party leader. In office, however, economists found that there was a considerable gulf between theory and practice.

The idea that a current budget deficit should be incurred in order to stimulate the economy was not entertained until the 1970s, when politicians became convinced that the correct way to tackle the problem of unemployment was through tax cuts and increased public spending. The 1978 budget, the most expansionary in the history of the state, was justified by the Keynesian argument that increased government spending would be the first stage of a process, the later stages of which would consist of the increased private-sector spending stimulated by the initial expansion. The results of this experiment in crude Keynesianism were disappointing. We enjoyed a spurt of exceptionally rapid economic growth in 1978 and 1979, but this was followed by no fewer than eight consecutive years of below average growth.[3]

By the early 1980s the borrowing which had funded this failed expansion had created a crisis in the national finances, and economists and politicians alike began to lecture the Irish people on their unrealistic expectations, overlooking for the moment the fact that politicians and at least some economists had combined to create such expectations in the first place. While politicians had implemented massive public spending programmes for electoral gain, now the electorate was told that a prosperous future required some short-term pain. Calls for cut-backs in public spending grew more and more vociferous as a monetarist economic philosophy became the order of the day and politicians competed with one another to preach the new orthodoxy. The electorate, understandably disillusioned, put an end to one-party majority governments, and an era of minority, coalition and inter-party governments took office, each blaming the previous administration for the plight of the nation's finances and the growing numbers unemployed.

In 1980 the then Taoiseach, Jack Lynch, stated that "a Taoiseach's place is out of office if unemployment in Ireland reached more than 100,000". Three years later the unemployment figure stood at over 200,000; three years after that over quarter of a million people were unemployed, and the talk in towns and villages was once more of emigration. With the unemployment figure rising inexorably, in mid-'93 the Minister of State for Labour Affairs, Mary O'Rourke, admitted that the problem would persist into the next century. This is hardly a record in which either politicians or economic planners can take pride.

The February 1993 Irish budget was presented as the new government's first step to tackle unemployment. Regretfully, I share the view that it fails utterly in this regard. In certain respects it is anti-job, particularly in its increase in VAT on clothing, as subsequent reaction in the retail trade confirms. More fundamental is the fact that in preparing budgets the Minister for Finance and his department are prisoners to the public debt. This is a severe constraint on policy, but it has also led to a particularly narrow, blinkered thinking. We have just gone through several years of strictly controlled budgeting to bring our national debt under control, yet, following the activity of currency speculators and the less-than-active support by our European partners during the recent crisis in the European Monetary System, a forced devaluation of the *púnt* added approximately £800 million to the public debt. At the same time, real interest rates in Ireland remain high and act as a major factor in reducing private investment in the economy.

The same logic which we had witnessed in the debate on entry into Europe came to the fore again in the debate on the Maastricht Treaty and the Single European Market which Ireland had been invited to join. But twenty years on some things had changed: there was now an almost monolithic consensus amongst politicians, economists and other leaders, that Ireland's only option was to follow the European programme. The public was told that failure to ratify the treaty would isolate Ireland from the rest of Europe – a claim which was quite invalid – and was promised a pot of gold, or £8 billion in structural funds, if the treaty was ratified without quibble. As in the debate twenty years previously, many observers quietly wondered if unqualified official acceptance of the European agenda revealed a covert understanding that Irish economic policy had failed, and that we would only survive with European support. Certainly the other countries of the Community felt free to display an independence of mind which was markedly lacking in Ireland.

Less than a year after ratifying the Maastricht Treaty, the effective collapse of the European Exchange Rate Mechanism (ERM) in August 1993 caused a frenzied debate on the very soundness of the Community. While Britain opted out of the

ERM, Ireland fought with considerable sacrifice to maintain the status of the *púnt* within the exchange rate system in the belief that the pain was worth being a part of Europe's monetary system. The fragile nature of this ambition was demonstrated when an army of speculators hacked the European dream apart in a matter of days.

In the context of the ERM there was always a gap between the rethoric and the reality. The nations which make up the European Community have different national policies because they have different national needs, which require different national solutions. In this scenario the goal of establishing a single currency without political integration was and is unrealistic.

The European ambition was rooted in the strength of the Franco-German alliance. As long as Germany was divided and the threat of a superpower in the East existed, that alliance was essential to West German economic interests, even if Germany had traditionally looked east rather than west. However, the portents of the weakening of the alliance were there, firstly in the several visits of the German Chancellor to the countries of eastern Europe and, secondly, in the demolition of the Berlin Wall, which refocused German policy towards the East. The high interest rate policy of the Bundesbank, which helped to unbalance the European currencies, was vital for German economic stability and was pursued with unshakeable conviction, even in the face of appeals to alter course.

The outcome was a serious setback to the whole EC ideal. In the aftermath of the currency crisis the Belgian Foreign Minister was quoted as saying: "The central purpose of Maastricht is dead. Protectionism will come back and will be the death knell of Europe. Europe is back to the drawing board." A professor from the London School of Economics remarked: "Everything we learned or knew before 1989 has to be jettisoned. New economic theories are needed."

The development of new ideas will not come easily to government and state planners who have adopted an almost entirely reactive rather than pro-active stance in Irish economic management. Delivering a lecture on Ireland's jobs crisis in early 1993, Harvard economist John Kenneth Galbraith urged the Irish government to look at the possibility of increasing public expenditure so as to stimulate economic growth and generate employment. He acknowledged that any increase in spending would result in a bigger deficit, but added:

For now, deficits should be accepted and, by government action and expenditure, put people to work. This in the short run will increase the public deficit and the public debt, attitudes to which have now reached paranoiac proportions. These attitudes must, for the time being, be ignored.[4]

As a leading world economist, Professor Galbraith's views are widely sought but, while I basically agree with his prescription, I can easily imagine it being viewed with alarm by politicians and administrators who have been engaged in a mission of financial orthodoxy since the late 1980s. Yet the government, and the economists who inform the government, might heed the remarks of former Commissioner Ray MacSharry, who points out in relation to the EC that the current malaise in the Community arises in large measure from its preoccupation with monetary policies, which have come to overshadow so many other areas which need attention. He pointed out, too, that Germany's Bundesbank exercised influence to the degree that other urgent issues, such as unemployment, immigration and subsidiarity, have been neglected. By the same token, Irish economic planners will have to look beyond the figures and statistics of economic performance and examine the factors underlying our failures – and our successes. In particular, it is time Irish governments stopped behaving like company receivers and assumed the mantle and responsibility of national managers. We have a crisis on our hands, but we cannot forever remain in crisis without putting forward solutions.

Notes

1. Garret FitzGerald, "Growth and Jobs: The Politics of Public Ambivalence", *The Jobs Crisis*, Mercier/RTE 1993

2. Figures for 1986

3. Brendan Walsh, "The Keynesian Legacy", *The Jobs Crisis*, Mercier/RTE 1993

4. John Kenneth Galbraith, "The Larger World Economy", op. cit.

Top of the Agenda

U NEMPLOYMENT IS NOT solved by throwing money at the problem; that much must be obvious. Between 1981 and 1990 a total of £1.4 billion was paid in cash grants to foreign and Irish-owned plants, and in that time 52,000 new jobs were created and 45,000 jobs were lost in these sectors; a nett gain of 7,000 jobs in ten years. Between 1973 and 1991 Ireland's total receipts from the EC budget amounted to £14.5 billion, yet we face the most serious unemployment crisis in our history. Ireland is set to receive a further £8 billion in structural funding from the EC, yet already leading economist Seán Barrett has warned that this transfer may yield very little in terms of employment.

Any strategy which aims to generate employment must reach to the nub of the question, and pursue its goals with vigour and determination. A Swedish study[1] which examines the problem in a number of different countries concludes that those which have consistently achieved low levels of unemployment share two fundamental characteristics: a consensus that full employment is of vital national importance, and institutions to put this national priority into effect. Neither of these factors have been much in evidence in Ireland, where political and administrative structures have fostered a kind of development which increased national wealth, but excluded many hundreds of thousands of people from any share in it.

In the first fifty years of independence we set up an incredible seventy plus semi-state or state sponsored bodies, about half of which were engaged in what can broadly be described as "development" activities. There was no compelling reason for each of these agencies, which were staffed initially by civil servants seconded from their previous posts, to be established as separate state bodies rather than form a special section within the relevant department. It is difficult to see why, for example, a separate Export Board was created, rather than develop an agency to monitor and promote exports in the existing department being developed, as is the case with the Board of Trade in the UK. Similarly I can see no logic in having a fisheries board, national or regional industries development authorities, training authorities or tourism board set up separately from the department which governs its activities. If additional expertise were required, it could have been brought in on a temporary basis or recruited on a more permanent basis as appropriate.

Abroad, many of these bodies grew to have separate high-priced, luxurious offices in various parts of the world, rather than sharing offices with one another or with diplomatic missions. At home they grew into separate bureaucracies, in many cases merely to monitor grant eligibility or the performance of firms which had obtained grants. Officers of these agencies called regularly on grant-aided firms to keep tabs on their progress towards achieving the targets for employment and sales predicted in their grant applications. Yet, as I point out below, a professional management structure had been introduced into local government which was perfectly capable of carrying out this task, and perhaps carrying it out more effectively.

If this sounds like an indictment of the quality of the public service, that is not my intention; what I am illustrating is the extent to which well-meaning but wrong decisions can flow from bad strategic planning. Nor is my criticism intended to disparage the undoubtedly excellent work done by agencies like Bord Fáilte, SFADCO, the IDA, ANCO and others, especially in the early, formative years of the state. However, I believe the same people could have done just as well within the state departmental structure, and that this structure could have avoided the need to spend *half* of all government grant support for economic development on the overhead costs of its administration.

Ironically, these semi-state bodies had been set up so as to circumvent the red tape and precedent-ridden procedure inherent in the country's government structure. Within the revolutionary leadership which won independence for Ireland, there was a wide diversity of vision as to the structure and character the new nation should adopt; the tragic civil war which followed independence scarred the growth of nationhood and created a political division which dominated debate in the first two decades after the Treaty. This, more than any other reason, prevented a deep-rooted review of the government and administrative structures we had inherited from the British. The Westminster precedent was not necessarily the only one nor the best for a nation of our size. In his excellent account of government and politics in Ireland, Professor Basil Chubb points out that "the essence of democracy is the participation of people in making or influencing the decisions that affect their lives."[2] Because we are a small island, a mere province in European terms, we need, as Chubb suggests,

> to examine the relevance of the structures of government we inherited from Great Britain. Small size and more intimate communities ought, in theory at least, to give opportunities for greater public participation in public affairs and make it easier for citizens to comprehend and identify with their government.

At local government level Ireland inherited a system which was largely based on suffrage for the landed classes. We adapted the system, to give it a wider voice, but did little until the County Management Act 1940 to introduce control by professional management. This came from the setting up of a Local Appointments Commission which was politically independent and, nationally, had sole power of appointment to all major local authority posts. Thus the power of local politicians to appoint "favourite sons", irrespective of their suitability, was eliminated and a much higher standard of qualification and expertise was evident in subsequent appointments. It is interesting to note that the precedent for this Act came from North America rather than Britain.

Local management had a much wider knowledge of their area than central government, a knowledge built on day-to-day contact and involvement. County managers had the incentive to build on the strengths of local communities and had, most probably, better prospects of encouraging local development programmes than either the government or semi-state sector, both of which lived at one remove from the regions. Having introduced professional management into local government, one might reasonably assume that the local authority structure would then be used to make the administration more accessible and responsive to local needs and aspirations. This was not how things turned out. In the style of administrative madness, central government progressively reduced the powers of local government over the succeeding years, diminishing its role to little more than a rubber stamp on central policy. The whole drift of policy was towards centralisation and, in turn, central government took on the character of what Basil Chubb describes as a democratic Leviathan,

> the kind of political system which is a product of long evolution and hard struggle, welfare-oriented, centralised, bureaucratic, tamed and controlled by competition among highly-organised elites, and, in the perspective of the ordinary citizen, somewhat remote, distant and impersonal. ...

> The politics of this new democratic Leviathan are above all the politics of compromise, adjustment, negotiation, bargaining; a politics carried out among professional and quasi-professional leaders who constitute only a small part of the total citizen body; a politics that reflects a commitment to the virtues of pragmatism, moderation and incremental change; a politics that is un-ideological and even anti-ideological.[3]

This system, and its governing ethos, marginalises small, rural and local communities. Its structure, as Professor Chubb points out, stresses

> the role of the representative (TD) as a contact man... with consequences not helpful to representative government. A system like the Irish tends to produce representatives who are parochial in character and outlook and who, for all their virtues in some respects, are not as well suited for the tasks of a national legislator as those conceived in other countries.[4]

Having first failed to use local administration as a means of bringing democracy down to grassroots level, the momentum of centralisation led in fact to a style of decision making which became more and more removed from democratic control. In discussing the decline of parliament in Ireland and Britain, its inability to be an effective critic of policy and a constructive force in government, Professor Chubb states:

> If Cabinet government (British style) belittles the role of the elected representative, so, more generally, does the general acceptance by western democracies of what Theodore Lowi has called the ideology of "interest group liberalism".... Policy is made and public affairs decided by ministers and their civil service advisors after consultation with the spokesmen of organised interest groups appropriate to the matter under review. These all-important meetings take place in the minister's room, the civil servant's office, the department's conference room; at this or that council, committee, and advisory or consultative body meeting. The spokesmen concerned are no doubt in some senses representative, but all this is a long way from the people's elected representative or from the representative assembly. In this system the contribution of the elected representative to the crucial stages of decision making... is peripheral.[5]

In my view, from the very beginning of the state we might usefully have considered a much stricter division of power between the legislature (Dáil and Senate), the administration (Government) and the judiciary (Courts of Law). The US and French models are worth study in this regard. For example, in the USA a directly elected President picks his cabinet of ministers from outside the elected assembly. The system of advice and consent ensures that the elected representatives have the right to veto the appointment, if the person has a record which in their view could adversely affect the national interest. In France the government is also chosen from outside parliament, though because of the greater parliamentary power in the French system, government ministers must reflect the views of the majority parties rather than the ideology of the president.

The appropriateness of each of these structures for an island of our size and population deserves careful study. Again, with a population approximately five percent of that of Great Britain, it was hardly axiomatic that the British models were the best ones on which to build an Irish democracy and ensure the participation of people in the making or influencing of decisions which affected their lives. Let me cite as a contrast one effect of the American system. In the directly elected legislatures and administrations at federal and state levels in the US, there have been many examples of a legislature dominated by one party with administration vested in the opposition. In turn, this has led, time and time again, to voting across party lines to promote more effectively the views of constituents. In other words, politicians have felt more responsible to their electorate than to their party.

A system of government which mandated the choice of government ministers from the ranks of elected deputies made a nonsense of any effective division of powers between the legislature and the administration. The dual role of ministers, at once representatives and administrators, led to policies being formulated with an eye to electoral gain, and largely framed to react to events rather than to create a climate for the healthy development of our nation. Faced with the present jobs crisis, for example, Ireland's politicians have been singularly unimpressive as leaders. Former Taoiseach Garret FitzGerald remarks:

There are five parties in the Dáil. This ought to be enough

to secure representation for the full spectrum of possible views on this most crucial national issue of unemployment. Yet those very measures which all informed opinion at home and abroad knows – and at least some people in all of our political parties privately accept – can alone make any real impact on unemployment seem to be taboo in that assembly.[6]

In the decision-making structure which developed, many policies were formulated on the basis of a narrow view of objectives without taking account of their impact in other areas. Transport policy is a case in point. Over the years, railways were subjected to economic assessment on a basis which was fundamentally flawed. The railway company had to bear the full cost of its entire structure, including maintenance of the permanent way, signalling, policing, housing, parking and rolling stock maintenance. Rail transport was then compared to the economics of road transport which, apart from road tax, did not take account of road construction, environmental damage, the cost of traffic lights, policing, parking and other essential provisions. As a result of this skewed comparison, we had the regrettable closure of the Harcourt Street line from Bray to Dublin and of a host of rural lines which formed part of the network. The Bray to Dublin closure is now recognised as a monumental blunder; the rail line closures in rural Ireland had an even more debilitating effect on rural communities and their ability to grow. If the railways had received a sizeable proportion of the funding given to roads, very many would have been saved, to the advantage of society as a whole.

National and local taxation policies provide further examples of blinkered policy-making. Clearly, tax has a major impact on economic development and job creation, and it is generally accepted that taxation policies formulated so as to gather revenue for the national coffers have had a negative effect on employment creation. Many of our mistakes in this area stem from Ireland's flawed management structure which too often simply ignored the adverse effects of its decisions. As a result, too many of our people feel estranged from the national decision-making process, and resentment of paying tax is at least partially an effect which flows from those feelings.

Industrial relations experts agree that the introduction of PAYE caused major strains in the relationship between employers and workers and, in many areas, gave rise to unrealistic wage demands. Most workers see their "take-home" pay as the sole reward they receive from their employers for their services, while few employers welcome the role of tax collector which can and does make them the immediate objective of worker frustration. I wonder if a stronger local taxation system, with a bias towards indirect taxation, might be more appropriate to the Irish psyche? If we delegated power and responsibility to local government and away from the centre, we would probably find it easier to introduce a taxation system which carried the wider consent of our people. At the very least, it would surely be better to examine every cause and effect factor of revenue requirement instead of merely tinkering with taxation policy in isolation.

In summary, because we failed after independence to examine adequately the structure of government and administration best suited to our small island country, we perpetuated a system more suited to a colonial power, one which absorbed more and more of the country's precious financial resources, generating a false dependency on illusory hopes and auction politics.

Subsidiarity is not just a new European catchphrase – it reflects the common sense of ensuring that people are given the maximum possible say in everything that affects their daily lives. Community is best built from the ground up; it cannot be imposed from the central government or its agencies. The most effective regional development undertaken in this country was in the Mid-West, and its success has been recognised both in Ireland and abroad. Its success was founded on the project being based in an identifiable area which saw itself as a community, and in having a regional authority, SFADCO, which believed in direct active participation in developing and promoting its region. If professional local authority managements had been more actively empowered and involved, they, too, would have been in a better position to review and assess the strengths and weaknesses of their local economies, as I suggest that community enterprise groups should now do. They would also have had a strong incentive, if only from the point of view of enlightened self-interest, to ensure that people participated in their work.

It is interesting to compare the Irish practice of formulating development policies in isolation from the community, in an atmosphere reflecting political aspirations more than concrete realities, with the Israeli example, which looked first to the roots of its situation. When Israel achieved nationhood, one of the earliest acts undertaken by the government was to carry out an audit of the strengths and weaknesses of the infant state. Where expertise was found to be lacking nationally, it resourced the best available experts money could buy. When we reflect on the Israeli miracle of turning the desert into a vineyard, of industries built from virgin soil, we should remember that this came largely from the use of imported expertise which was used to develop and train native entrepreneurs and co-operatives in the planning, design and skills required. To a limited extent Ireland did the same when we implemented the Shannon Hydro-Electric Scheme and set up the Irish Sugar Company's beet processing plants in the 1920s. However, unlike Israel, we did not undertake a thorough assessment of our worth. Such an analysis would have forced us to test the validity of our image of Ireland as a poor, isolated island and of letting the thinking of the pre-independence administrations take root in our development policies. To one degree or another, its lack led us to accept the inevitability of conditions as they were. We had at least two excellent opportunities to rectify our failure in this regard: firstly when we adopted a policy of self-sufficiency in the 1930s and secondly when we adopted the Whitaker Programmes for Economic Expansion. If part of the budget for these programmes had been devoted to such an audit, we would have gained a clearer understanding of how to go about developing the resources of our ecomomy.

We are all familiar with the unflattering comparisons made between agricultural development in Ireland as against that in Holland and Denmark. But if these criticisms are justified, why has our national planning for so long ignored the basic weaknesses which lie at their foundation? Why, too, has it taken until now to assess our potential in horticulture, fishing, mariculture, food processing, forestry etc? Was there room to focus on areas of processing a wider range of actual or potential natural assets for sale in international markets? These are the kinds of questions which any professional management audit of "Ireland Inc." would seek to answer. They are also the questions which any competent management of "Ireland Inc." ought to have addressed in the past two decades or more. Yet I fear it is likely that in fact some of the agreements we have negotiated in Brussels may have restricted our ability to develop the potential of these assets in the future.

Now, of course, the major problem the country faces, one which will test our resources to the full, is the crisis of unemployment. What exactly has "putting unemployment to the top of the political agenda" really meant?

The Culliton Report[7] is the document for salvation most frequently quoted in current debates on unemployment and referred to by politicians and planners as the touchstone of Ireland's employment creation programme. This report, submitted on 1 January 1992, is very largely concerned with infrastructural development and is necessarily medium to long-term in nature. The very first paragraph of the preface sets the tone so far as unemployment is concerned:

We have concluded that there are no short term solutions, no quick fixes and no soft options left. We found no unused cash reservoir which could be tapped to provide early sustainable jobs...

It is a time for change. Time to realise that Governments on their own cannot provide us with permanent secure jobs and a growing standard of living... Time to accept that the solutions to our problems lie in our own hands.... The next decade will provide greater opportunities for enterprise and initiative. The extent to which our community will accept the challenge will determine our future levels of employment and national wealth.[8]

The particular challenge we are being asked to accept – to show enterprise and initiative – is not clearly defined, and neither does the report put forward concrete proposals to show how the enterprise and initiative of our communities should be supported over the next ten years or so. Yet in a later chapter entitled "A Vision of Irish Industry in the Year 2000" the report states that: "The ultimate success of our strategy will, inevitably, tend to be measured by its ability to address the unemployment crisis." It goes on:

But the net growth from jobs from industry and private service, could not realistically be expected to average more than 10,000 per year and that would be a considerable achievement. Such a contribution will not be negligible, but it will not be able to absorb a labour force at the rate it will still be growing unless emigration resumes on a large scale.[9]

No solution without large-scale emigration?

In fairness to Culliton and his committee, their brief was limited by specific terms of reference:

To review and make recommendations on industrial policy in Ireland and on public policy generally as it affects industrial development. The review should address, particularly, the internationally trading indigenous industrial sector and, where possible, identify policies and measures... which would form the basis for the development of this sector over the medium to long term, with a view to increasing employment and wealth creation. For this purpose, industry includes internationally traded services.[10]

Within the framework of these very specific terms of reference, the report puts forward many excellent recommendations on taxation, infrastructure, education, support for industry, state institutional change and so on. For these, its authors deserve congratulation. However, the majority of these proposals could only be implemented in a medium-to-long-term time frame. But the committee had no brief to address the specific and immediate problem of unemployment. Contrary to some misguided political and media debate and comment, the early introduction of the Culliton recommendations is neither feasible nor an answer to our present unemployment crisis.

For these reasons I find puzzling the inclusion of a section headed "The Problems of Unemployment". This includes such statements as: "unemployment is likely to increase significantly in the coming years" and "industrial growth can contribute through provision of jobs. But more direct action is necessary", and "unemployment is a problem to which the solution can only be long term".

These statements are of no real help in addressing what is accepted as a national crisis of very grave magnitude. With the exception of correctly drawing our attention to the need to follow the lead of other countries "by reducing the burden of labour legislation for smaller firms until they reach reasonable size", there is very little in this section which can usefully contribute to the present debate. The report briefly refers to re-designing the income support for unemployed along the lines of the Swedish model, and to including more pro-active re-training and job placement components. But what precise re-training do they suggest and for what jobs? All that follows is the suggestion that "the Area-Based initiative of the PESP offers some hope in this direction..." and "given the high degree of labour mobility, it is important not to fall behind the UK in this regard". Quite frankly, having so slavishly imported the failed policies of our UK neighbour, we have little cause for concern.

The Programme for Economic and Social Progress (PESP) was adopted by the social partners in 1991 in an effort to address national social and economic problems generally. It also represents the search for a new model with which to achieve greater

progress towards employment growth. Section VII of that programme – "Area-Based Response to Long-Term Unemployment" – sets out the character of this new model. In paragraph
1, it defines its role as one "designed to implement a community response in particular local areas. The proposed strategy,"
it goes on, "will have local communities as the primary
movers," and it lists the Community Enterprise Programme
specifically as one of the four components of enterprise development. In these statements the PESP programme follows very
closely the European Commission's consistent advocacy of
genuine community empowerment. The PESP itself was meant
to recognise the unique contribution each sector could make
to furthering the development of the community, and was
supported by the EC on those terms.

In several discussions in the European Parliament, Commission representatives have emphasised the overriding need for
development policies to have a broad level of community as-
sent, trust and support. It follows from this that one of the central criteria for measuring the success or failure of any
partnership programme is the degree to which the community
being served accepts the programme as a meaningful influence in its daily life. This sense of involvement is best achieved
by the presentation of a programme which will be, and will be
seen to be, supportive of a wide range of individual and community self-help and job creation initiatives. No single person,
agency or group has a monopoly on solutions to the problems
of unemployment and social deprivation, and none has the
prescriptive right to give its individual or group interests priority over the fundamental rights and needs of others. On this
basis we can develop a logical series of principles which must
govern all partnership policy if it is to create real partnership.
These include:

  * A clear recognition that the partnership is established to
  promote a community-based response to long-term unemployment.
  * A recognition that there are many diverse but compatible

enterprise development programmes which can and should co-exist in any specific community area. Each requires resources to encourage and assist development and expansion.

* There must be a clear commitment to support the work of all programmes in an even-handed fashion and encouragement must be given to all interested groups who have a positive role to play.

* Both the PESP and EC programmes accept and encourage positive discrimination in favour of areas of greatest deprivation and need. To follow this principle through in practice, a high level of resources must be allocated to enterprise groups establishing a community-based response to the needs of disadvantaged areas.

* It is fundamental to the achievement of genuine partnership that policy is designed to enable positive development to emerge. This can only come about by giving individual and collective community initiatives support, encouragement and resources.

* It is paramount to harmonious community development that no one community group be allowed to assume or be allotted a dominant role in enterprise development.

How has the implementation of the partnership policies under the PESP measured up to these criteria? In its application for European funding to support community-inspired employment initiatives, the government claimed:

The purpose of the grant is to support the development of indigenous potential at a local level. It will focus on measures which encourage and support local economic development initiatives, stimulate new economic activity and support for local community-based socio-economic development. In particular, the grant will aim to support and tap fully local enterprise initiatives and to promote integrated economic, social and community development of local areas. It will aim to support the main forces of local development by providing funds to develop local leadership capacity where required.

This attempts to convey the government's support for a policy of community empowerment but expertly avoids confronting the core issue. It refers to eligible bodies as the twelve area-based partnerships set up under the PESP programme, other local community bodies, a special travellers' education and development group and – rather vaguely – private promoters. The EC grant is to be managed by an intermediary company set up or designated by the Irish government; this is not unreasonable, provided the company acts independently of the government in administering the funds.

However, the area partnerships, as set up, are staffed by persons recruited or seconded from the state agencies. The boards and sub-groups consist of state agency officers and persons handpicked by them but defined as community representatives. The bulk of the first EC grant to the partnerships was allocated to projects previously funded by the state agencies, whose staff now man the community partnership boards. The balance of the funding was absorbed in the creation of a new tier of bureaucracy.

In 1992 I participated in a discussion with some officers of the European Directorate-General for Regional Policies in which one officer was sharply critical of the Irish use of European funds. He felt the Irish government had a policy of centralising power and denying effective regionally-inspired initiatives for economic and social development. The view was expressed that the Irish government was using European funding to facilitate cut-backs in Irish spending rather than to generate new programmes. During this discussion a UK colleague reminded me of a proposal which we had jointly submitted to a government minister in the 1980s, for a pilot programme in Dublin centre city, similar to a UK initiative which had attracted significant EC support. Our proposal was rejected because it might create a precedent for local projects successfully by-passing central government's control of all EC funding. More recently I had sight of correspondence from the Directorate-General which would suggest its unhappiness with the lack of genuine community representation under the present programme.

All of this is cold comfort to the vast numbers of people trying to deal with the havoc unemployment has wreaked in their lives and those of their families. It provides little consolation to depressed regions and communities or to the host of Irish businesses struggling to survive in a contracting marketplace.

There is no simple, overnight solution to the problems besetting the Irish economy, nor any single economic theory which will light the path to prosperity. However, the first step in our journey of self-development is to recruit the human resources of the nation. To do this we must create the climate for positive, action-oriented measures.

The concept of effective community empowerment needs to be explored and acted on. With the support of the European Community, whose Commission has long advocated a more balanced partnership between local communities and the centre, we can and must encourage the rapid development of community-based enterprise. Such a strategy will help to wean us away from our reliance on a "big brother" figure who will take care of our problems for us, and can be the force which allows us recover control of our local economies.

Notes

1. Goran Therborn, *Why Some People Are More Unemployed than Others*, Verso 1987
2. Basil Chubb, *The Government and Politics of Ireland*, OUP 1970, p.313
3. Ibid. p.320
4. Ibid. p.319
5. Ibid.
6. *The Irish Times* July '93; Dr FitzGerald's measures differ from those outlined in this book; nonetheless the point stands.
7. "A Time for Change: Industrial Policy for the 1990s. Report of The Industrial Policy Review Group." Government Publications, 1992

8. Ibid. p.7
9. Ibid. p.24
10. Ibid. p.17

Community Initiative

ROBERT JUNGK, professor of economics at Berlin University, wrote: "Initiatives inspired directly by the people are probably the laboratories in which the twenty-first century is and will be developed." I would go one step further and say that the initiative must not only come from the people, but must also be implemented by them.

It is widely accepted today that we need to take radical new steps to combat the growing incidence of deprivation and disadvantage in our society, and that much of this deprivation is rooted in unemployment, in people being deprived of gainful work. Our main concern is with the high levels of unemployment among the young, the unskilled and the long-term unemployed. There are others factors, too, which lead to economic and social disadvantage – the absence of skills, low pay, lack of personal mobility, low levels of economic activity and educational achievement, inadequate community and leisure facilities and, often, sub-standard housing and environmental conditions.

The key objective of community enterprise is to develop a community response to this deprivation and disadvantage, to plan and implement a job creation and community revitalisation strategy for any given area. There is no grand design or plan which will be effective in each and every community – needs, habits, resources and aspirations vary quite dramatically from place to place. The task of repairing and strengthening the community economy so as to provide new job opportunities and promote long-term community development is not a simple one, and the means, too, are both diverse and complex. Local knowledge, backed up by research, analysis and planning, is fundamental in choosing the best strategy.

This cannot and will not happen by accident: the initiative must come from people in the community. Those who take the first step must gather a small group of other concerned people, and sit down to talk about their community and the direction it might take. They must attempt to visualise the realistic potential of their area in economic and social terms, a process which very often starts by recognising that there are problems which can destroy the community's future if they are not attended to.

Some years ago I was asked at a lecture I was giving to just such a group, how I could see any small community being able to take effective action to turn the tide of regional and national events which affected their lives. I asked the group to step outside the present for a moment and imagine that a nuclear Armageddon had occured, but that they had somehow survived. In this scenario there is no local or state structure to give them aid. Would they die without it? I didn't think so. Necessity would force one or more people in the group to assume leadership, and the group as a whole would work to ensure its own survival. When they had overcome their immediate problems, they would naturally seek out other survivors, firstly in the neighbouring areas, later in a wider region. But this would be of little use unless they had organised themselves to a point where they had something more than sympathy to offer to their fellow survivors. Of course, if they believed they were strong enough they could on the other hand try to impose their dominance on the other surviving communities, but having already suffered so terribly from the effects of man's inhumanity to man, we might hope that they would reach out to their neighbours in peace and the spirit of love and charity.

Back in the present, we – each and every one of us – see unemployment and the social deprivation which follows it spreading like a cancer through our communities, destroying our hopes and dreams for ourselves and for our children. Instead of asking what "they" are doing about it (and at this stage we might agree that "they" are not doing enough, nor are they likely to of their own volition), we must ask: what can I do, what can you do, what can we as a caring community do in search of a remedy? We will find that there is no strength to do anything until we come together, but if we do combine our collective resources, our skills and ideas and energy, we can make real progress.

There are many examples of how effective such community action can be and has been in other spheres of activity. Take an apparently simple one, like the tidy towns initiative. Organised by Bord Fáilte, the tidy towns competition is a good example of the positive results which can flow from a genuine partnership between the state and local communities; it is also an excellent example of the power of local organisation and endeavour. While Bord Fáilte provided the incentive, thousands of local communities throughout the length and breadth of Ireland worked long hours planning improvements in their environment, and implementing them. In all of these communities the local people had to learn to understand the different components which went into creating a pleasant environment; the organisers for their part had to overcome apathy, generate teamwork, find and promote a common vision of how the community might be, and work to a plan that was, and was seen to be, achievable. There were very many doubting Thomases when this competition was first started, but anyone who has travelled around Ireland in the last ten years or so cannot fail to recognise the change which has taken place in the visual appearance of our towns and villages. These results show that the ability to come together and co-operate at local level is still very much alive, despite the corroding influence of state paternalism. And this kind of community spirit is vital if we are to begin to launch a successful offensive against the evils of unemployment and social decay.

Change is desparately needed if we are, as John F. Kennedy said, to have any chance of writing history rather than merely reading it. Structural political change, too, is necessary, but government and central bureaucracy will always see problems in the context of a national or international canvass; the subtle detail within the picture is best seen at local level. As author Evelyn Waugh points out, "In small communities quantitive judgements do not apply; a single gesture to alleviate pain is enough reason to act." Neither will politicians be forced into the necessary structural change unless communities of people exert pressure on them to do so. Such pressure will have all the more authority if it comes from strong, assertive communities, communities which know their rights because they have worked to right themselves. To do this local groups must learn the essential components of community initiative, and must know the concept which lies behind community action and the strategy which will help to implement this concept successfully.

The first objective is to recover control over our own lives by recovering control over our local economy. The farming communities did this throughout Ireland in an earlier era by establishing co-operatives; others in towns, villages and cities used the credit union concept to restore some control over ordinary people's finances; still more demonstrate the effectiveness of co-operation in sport and cultural organisation. In all these cases a shared vision unlocked the dynamic of people's energy, and set it to work within the circle of a community

To build a common vision of how our locality might be developed, we need first of all to look around at what we have and what we lack. The community enterprise group's work begins with research which draws a picture of the local economy in its entirety. It looks at how the community as a whole gains its income and how it spends it; it examines the needs of the community with the aim of identifying how these needs can be met locally; and it gathers together a register of all the skills which the community possesses. All of these economic elements are audited, the information gathered in a comprehensive bank of knowledge which helps the enterprise group to see where it might begin to act so as to influence the local situation to the advantage of the community.

If we learn to source our needs locally, to the maximum extent that we can, then we have recovered control of the local economy. Examples abound, if only because most localities spend huge sums of money each year on goods purchased from outside. When a community enterprise group carried out a rough "energy audit" in two Welsh parishes, it found that they were spending some £250,000 a year on "imported" energy. On the basis of this information the group began to look around for ways to reduce this outflow of spending, and were soon investigating ideas to develop an insulation programme in the area. The idea very quickly became an employment-creating enterprise, and resulted in a quite dramatic saving to individual households and the community as a whole.

A comprehensive community audit which covers the whole of the community's income and expenditure will reveal that a range of products and services which are purchased outside the community could in fact be provided locally. Essentially, this research highlights how local spending supports or fails to support local, regional or national jobs. It is often surprising how little aware people are of what they buy. A north Dublin programme, located in an area renowned for its vegetable-growing, was taken aback when its research found that almost all the produce in the local supermarkets was imported. Regardless of its price tag, an imported product can be a very expensive buy if it contributes to unemployment; it also damages oneself, by diminishing one's earning power and causing one's community environment to deteriorate. Government cannot discriminate in favour of home-produced goods without offending EC regulations, but, with our individual freedom of choice, we can and must: a "buy local" approach generates the revenue which creates local employment.

While this research will help to show how spending can be redirected for local benefit, the community enterprise group can also carry out a specific "needs analysis". By talking to local people and getting them to talk to one another about services or products they feel they are lacking, the community can begin to identify common needs which may be met by a little local organisation and enterprise. This proposition can be difficult to pin down, but careful research will help the group make intelligent choices between the different and varied ideas which this discussion brings to light. In a housing estate in Dublin with a big population of young married people, one need that emerged in a group discussion was that couples found it difficult to take a holiday because they were caring for an elderly relative and felt anxious at leaving them alone. A group of nurses who lived locally responded, and set up a "short stay" residence which looked after the older folk for a couple of weeks or even just a few days at a time. The initiative provided work for young women who might otherwise have emigrated, and made a real contribution to the quality of local people's lives. There are ideas of all kinds latent in every community, and new ideas for products or services can also be discovered by specific research in established sources.

Money, ideas and products are important, but a community's greatest asset is its people. What do you really know about the people of your area? If an enterprise group is to work for the community, it must first find out who they are, how many are employed or unemployed, and it must record the kinds of skills and aptitudes which are found locally. This survey registers the human resources of the community. Armed with this information the enterprise group can approach local employers, pointing out the type of skills available to them; it can also offer businesses the use of ideas generated by the group's research. If local businesses expand as a result of taking on these ideas, a condition of their exploiting them can be that they employ local labour from the community register.

The register helps also to identify potential entrepreneurs for start-up businesses; it provides the essential briefing material for effective negotiation with state, semi-state or EC agencies; and it becomes the basis for targeted job placement, negotiations with potential businesses attracted as inward investment, and a guide for retraining needs. At a later stage it provides the information needed to match the human skills of the community with the potential business ideas provided by transfering business innovation and technology from large-scale enterprise or technology centres to local community enterprise. In the meantime, the information gathered by the enterprise initiative can also be collated and published in a directory of local trades, services and businesses which is circulated to every household.

When a community group begins this quite far-reaching research, it is bound to meet responses locally which vary from enthusiasm to suspicion. But the primary issue in community enterprise is to explore what we, the people, can do to restore control over our community's destiny. Can we or can't we play a part in reducing unemployment and social want? Very many of the old approaches no longer work: the days when education and qualifications guaranteed a secure job are gone, the days of grants and hand-outs are virtually over, and if people really want to achieve something positive in their communities they must begin to do it themselves. If this is to happen the community must come together, with the aim of developing to the full what are, after all, its own assets.

The enterprise group's research aims simply to discover these assets and weigh their value. It does not just count local income, nor reveal who owns what locally. Its purpose is to look all the time for opportunities for local enterprise, for new ideas and proposals, and it tries not just to measure the status quo but to open up options for the future. The very process of encouraging people to put their heads together, to think about their livelihoods and the life of their locality, brings tremendous benefits in itself. People begin to think and talk about what they might do, ideas which may have lain dormant for years are rekindled. Subtle changes make themselves felt, slowly perhaps, but surely. Choices are made in the shops; the new home-owner discovers that just a few streets away is a carpenter who makes surprisingly inexpensive furniture and a fabric shop which can run those curtains up in no time. The community's skills and talents, whatever they may be, are brought to life by being brought to people's attention. And an environment which welcomes initiative, even demands it, encourages more from its members.

If good ideas and people are combined with adequate capital and management, job creation will follow. The aim of the community enterprise group is to bring together these ingredients in the community, and so begin a process which will lead to the starting and nurturing of new businesses and the expansion of existing ones. The small business initiative, whether a fifteen- to twenty-person private firm, a five person co-operative or a single self-employed person, is the life-blood of any local economy. Small businesses play a vital role in rebuilding communities, and a local economy built on small businesses is better able to withstand fluctuations in the national and international economy. In the recent past we have seen entire communities, in Ireland and elsewhere, devastated by the closure of one large enterprise which was the area's principal employer.

However, the failure rate of individual small businesses is also extremely high – reaching as much as 90% of new start-ups. What is needed, then, is a network to support the small business economy. It is not too much to imagine that every locality might have a network to care for and nourish the local small business community; in turn, it will help care for and nourish the locality. All local economies try to retain existing business, to facilitate new ones, to attract outside investment and to foster a climate which supports enterprise. But by doing this work consciously and methodically, the community enterprise approach increases the likelihood of success, and all the time its objective is to create jobs for local residents and to give purpose and support to the re-training and placement of the unemployed.

The community enterprise group fosters employment initiatives by circulating information and ideas within the community, and it also supports people with ideas for business or self-employment either by providing professional business advice and counselling, or by helping people with ideas to find the information and services they need. The Dublin-based initiative, Success, mentioned in the Introduction, was started by a group of just six people, and has grown to encompass a programme which now provides seed capital and professional business advice for local entrepreneurs. Communities such as this, which are able to raise funds for enterprise initiatives, have had significant successes, while less fortunate communities have had to work hard to overcome their relative disadvantages.

Every enterprise group must raise what it can from the community itself, and set up a working group to investigate all other potential sources of finance. With funding at its disposal the enterprise group may provide capital directly to the entrepreneur or unemployed person setting up in self-employment, though this is rarely done; more often, the group helps people to access capital from programmes such as the PESP and LEADER, philantropic bodies and trusts, state grant aid, and other sources. Employment and enterprise opportunities are also created by targeting ideas which provide opportunities for local businesses to expand, encouraging new business start-ups and, in some instances, through directly establishing businesses by forming community companies or co-operatives. The community can also engage in joint ventures with people who have the ideas, skills and competence to establish self-employing or business initiatives. All the time the community enterprise group is working to identify and support enterprise initiative within the community.

The two goals of community enterprise – to create job opportunities and revitalise the social fabric of the community – are distinct and this distinction must be recognised in practice, though at the same time, of course, the two strands link together to strengthen the community's social and economic base. The enterprise programme aims to promote the development of economic enterprise in the community, and does so on business-like terms. Though it may be put in place by the voluntary work of the enterprise group, the support service to business must be fully professional, either by employing a full-time business advisor or referring potential entrepreneurs to professional skills – legal, accounting, marketing, engineering etc. – when they need them. The people who use these services pay for them. The enterprise programme is a self-sustaining project.

One of the major reasons for the uneconomic development of community initiatives in Ireland and parts of the UK has been the failure to separate community support programmes from community enterprise. A support programme includes job matching, placement and training, and personal counselling to help re-build the confidence of people whose lives have been ruined by long periods of unemployment. In this work the community enterprise group also has a key role, as effective community co-operation provides the organisation, incentive and will to counter social deprivation by social action. The vision of people who come together to set up a community enterprise group, many of whom may be securely employed and not likely to benefit directly from the project, extends beyond the materialistic; theirs is very often a vision of a community which cares about its members and uses its resources for their benefit.

This social or ethical philosophy is in no way detached from the aims of promoting enterprise initiatives so as to foster employment. The social and physical revival of a community plays, in turn, a large part in promoting its economic development, through identifying and encouraging the skills found in the community and through improving its social and physical environment, all of which make the area a more attractive one in which to live, work, and invest. Thus the group helps to organise plans for environmental improvement, non-commercial employment schemes, leisure facilities and activities, disadvantaged minority support initiatives; to help improve the level of skills in the local population, the enterprise group can organise second-chance education or specific training programmes in co-operation with local schools or through Outreach programmes. The community can raise funds for these social developments, but usually they require permanent subsidy and must be financed either by charitable donation or state funding.

This level of intervention in the community demands commitment, though no more than is given at present to sporting, cultural and political activities throughout the country. The work of community enterprise organisation can be undertaken by voluntary staff, using the skills of local people trained by participation in seminars or by hands-on experience. Professional guidance helps to get things done more quickly and full or part-time workers, some of whom can perhaps be recruited through social employment schemes, relieve the burden on community activists. In the USA and Europe great progress is achieved at community level because community development programmes are given grants in aid to pay for professional input in support of voluntary effort – in fact, in some cases the professional is expected to produce a blueprint of what can be achieved in the locality, and this in turn has led to wider local support for development plans. Such back-up and a professionally developed community business plan are often essential if the community is to be considered for grants for building, training, technology transfer etc. at a later stage.

In Ireland, consultancy support grants when they are available are rarely adequate to cover the cost of employing professionals, and the only other support on offer is the occasional appointment by FÁS of a local enterprise worker at a salary scale which is derisory to the qualified professional. This lack of positive support has been a source of much frustration to community groups who have come together to organise initiatives in their localities. Their lack of experience, and the lack of professional guidance, has caused many groups to concentrate on a narrow element of the community concept, and as a result they fail to develop the much broader programme of community enterprise which, in its scope and depth, builds a more solid foundation for future development.

Even so, local organisation, starting at amateur level, can do an immense amount of work and bring enormous benefit to the community, as has been the case in Tallaght and many other places where a local initiative has been tried. Yet as the community enterprise organisation becomes an essential local institution, it will require at least some full-time paid staffing. Over time volunteers will have acquired confidence in their abilities, and the experience they have gained will in most cases qualify them to take on a professional role. While the needs and the successes of each area will vary, within a few years of starting off most communities will have tapped sufficient local enterprise to be in a position to found an enterprise centre to house start-up businesses: unlike the state, the community organisation should always foster enterprise before housing it, rather than create an enterprise centre and then cast round for tenants. The enterprise group should also be able to run a resource centre to help place local people, both young and old, in employment. The resource centre offers regular counselling for actual or potential business ventures, and has access to legal, patenting, engineering and other relevant expertise. In addition, the group will probably have set up community companies or co-operatives in either manufacturing or services to meet some of the local or regional needs which were uncovered by the initial local research.

The community must build its own strength before it can look for and make commitments to other communities, business enterprises and organisations, but as community enterprise organisations grow they begin to contribute effectively to regional and national development. The community which has demonstrated its ability to manage itself and its ability to provide economic skills will be an attractive location for inward investment. The community enterprise group, for its part, takes on a more sophisticated managerial role. Now it might undertake research to assess the business developments which can be achieved in the area over the next three to ten years, to analyse the skills which will be needed to facilitate that development, and to set up training programmes to train people in those skills. A project in East London, for example, attracted some sizeable entrepreneurs into the area by offering to provide them with precisely the categories and numbers of skilled workers they required. The community group must also encourage large companies sited in or near the community to assist the development organisation. In the UK this liaison with local companies persuaded them to source goods and services locally, to second qualified personnel to assist the community enterprise organisation, to provide unused accommodation at favourable terms, and to put money into soft-loan funding for new business ventures.

Community enterprise groups can combine, nationally and internationally, to exchange ideas and information, and work with innovation, technology or business centres to access innovative ideas and new technologies. Earlier we mentioned the energy audit undertaken in two parishes in Wales. Energy options are only one area that benefit from a search for alternative ways of meeting human needs in a new and better way, due to the constant drain on non-renewable sources of energy. There is a great deal of interest world-wide in manufacturing fuel from organic sources, by turning the oil from plants or the gas from sewage and waste into fuel. At present the technology for converting these raw materials is being researched in universities and other institutes, and many fuel products are just beginning to come on the market – in a French programme, buses are run on fuel processed from trees. New technologies create new opportunities. In this case, for example, the opportunity for farmers to use land which might otherwise be underutilised (or set aside under the CAP) to grow crops for conversion into fuel. And while community enterprise groups will almost always start in a small way, looking at local needs in a local context, further down the line there is the potential to grasp just such new and exciting innovations and become a part of their development, when local resources are linked to technical advances and put new and useful products on the market.

Co-operatively, community initiative creates the political imperative for a national, rather than local assessment of resources, and for funding to be correctly targeted so as to develop them. In addition they will have created the environment in which the provision of resources to the modern enterprise community is an economically viable reality. All of this work, and all the elements of the modern enterprise community, follow in a natural progression from the very first stage of community organisation. All of it can only be built, brick upon brick, by the work of individual communities.

The community enterprise organisation is the nexus of the community's needs and potential. Its authority comes directly from a community which decides to act together to achieve its goals. To sustain interest and momentum in community-based initiatives, a number of elements are essential. The first is educating local communities to the possibilities of their area and the processes necessary to develop a meaningful community programme. To do this successfully a dynamic, almost missionary approach is needed, and the people who establish the community enterprise initiative must supply this dynamic. This is an ongoing process throughout the early years of any initiative.

A second component is the careful selection and training of both trustees and community leaders to head up the effort. All of us are gifted with different talents and should be encouraged to put our different abilities to work for the benefit of the community, but whatever our role, the skills we offer should give no grounds whatever for a feeling or inferiority or superiority. Leadership roles, in particular, should be taken on as a burden, not assumed as an honour. The politics of power is fatal to this process; indeed, the achievement of Episcopalian and Lutheran groups in promoting social revitalisation in urban communities in the USA points to the advantage of an altruistic or Christian influence.

The energy of this initiative must be organised in a structure which touches and influences the community at all levels. Initially the organisation must be largely voluntary. It is headed by an executive committee which is elected by the members of the enterprise group. Working groups take on the task of local research, carrying out surveys of skills, resources and needs; investigating questions of finance, premises and other specific issues which must be addressed. Ultimately the aim of these groups' work is to produce a comprehensive community plan based on their research, and the community enterprise group then decides on the best way to organise itself to begin the work of putting these aims into effect. This permanent organisation, the community enterprise group formed in the style of a company or friendly society, must then oversee the implementation of the plan.

In an era of increasingly constrained central government and local resources, strategies which can provide creative and practical solutions to local needs must be developed. If government needs to redefine its role, in turn the private sector, and communities in particular, need to look realistically at what they, too, can contribute. Clearly they cannot be expected to make good government cuts in public spending, nor to generate new public spending programmes. But the local community, including local enterprise, must be willing to commit money and effort to a programme of community development if it is to have any chance of success.

Experience in the USA suggests that the key to unlock local initiative is the community enterprise approach, which has an unrivalled ability to harness the potential energy and vitality of a new kind of public/private sector partnership. In response to the racial riots of the 1960s and '70s, big business, municipalities, state governments and the churches were forced to re-evaluate where the profit-driven economy was leading society. The concepts of big being better, of profit overriding the rights of human beings, of communities being irrelevant in the global schemes of business, all required a sharp rethink. From that rethink emerged a compromise which recognised that community stability was probably better served by small business units providing rewarding local employment than by big business and mobile capital. Thus communities, business, local and federal authorities, often with church groups acting as catalysts for or trustees of the development, co-operated in programmes designed to reclaim the local economy by developing small business and community venture initiatives. A degree of success was achieved in the places where it was tried, and, however limited, the outcome clearly pointed the way to achieving a more stable community life. The real tragedy was, and is, that big business would only participate in community programmes when it saw its self interest would also be served.

The purpose of this kind of partnership between communities, local authorities, semi-state bodies and the state itself, is to ensure that policy decisions are taken only after full consultation and are implemented so as to cause the minimum possible disruption to the lives of the people affected. In this way the participants contribute to the benefit of the broader community while promoting their own individual or organisational interests. The state recognises this in its interaction with and support of large business and pressure groups. Substantial areas of community life also benefit from, and in certain instances require partnership. The local economy, community services, the neighbourhood, each involves economic and political factors that are neither exclusively private nor wholly public.

There are many simple examples to illustrate this practice of real partnership. Some years ago when we suffered very heavy snowfalls, many residents' groups and community organisations took on the task of clearing snow from pathways and shopping forecourts so as to help the overloaded local authority service concentrate on clearing the roads. Many community and voluntary groups at present engage in reclaiming re-us-able resources from waste, organising their activities to ensure that what is left for dumping is collated for easy handling by the waste disposal authorities. Voluntary visits to the aged and infirm reduce the workload on an overstretched Health Board community service. There are many examples of third-level institutes, professional training bodies and churches providing Outreach or distance education programmes to remote communities which would otherwise be unable to enjoy such services. In a planning case in a Dublin suburb, where a planned development offended local residents, the community group avoided confrontation by persuading the local authority to offer an exchange of sites so that the development could go ahead in an area where it found a greater welcome. The practice of effective co-operation helps create a situation where different demands can be satisfied, whereas confrontation is destructive to all the parties concerned.

Many years ago a dedicated garda officer warned that unless there was a considerable increase in funding to fight drug pushing, the drugs problem in Ireland would grow to epidemic proportions. Sadly, subsequent events have proved him right. Are we to wait for the inevitable explosion of anger which rising levels of unemployment will bring to our society before the state wakes up to its responsibilities? Despite our much-vaunted Christianity, concern for the unemployed seems to be a low priority for a society which is too often self-centred, unconcerned with its neighbour's difficulty. What has happened to the idealism that motivated the founders of our nation? To cherish all of the children of the nation was not, for them, merely a pious aspiration, but a real objective.

Today we face a challenge as serious as any we have faced in our history. Without speedy and radical new initiatives, unemployment will continue to increase and politicians may soon be unable to use tax-funded welfare and other benefit mechanisms to diminish its impact. The late Cardinal Dalton once warned that the crust of civilisation is very thin. We need only look at the violence which exists on our island to recognise the truth of that warning. Unless we reverse sharply the current growth in unemployment and get back to a point where the elimination of involuntary unemployment can be realistically visualised, violence becomes a very real, very frightening prospect. We can only avoid this drift towards anarchy if we move swiftly to restore control over our own destiny. This demands concerted action, firstly at community level in initiatives which unite employed and unemployed alike, developing into genuine community empowerment and a sustained national partnership between communities and government.

Action Tallaght

SHORTLY AFTER RETURNING from working abroad I was approached by the Society of St Vincent de Paul with a request to carry out a brief survey of the north Dublin suburb of Tallaght and present a plan for the area's revitalisation. The organisation, which undertakes charitable programmes in socially deprived areas, briefed me on the situation.

The area had been developed in the late 1960s and early '70s on the basis of the "newtown" planning precedent set in the UK and elsewhere. It was planned as a model town, where housing, shopping facilities, office complexes and industrial estates would all be constructed in a well-serviced and pleasant environment. In Tallaght, however, the concept went horribly wrong. The planners had initiated a phased programme of first housing businesses and then building estates to accommodate the new workforce which they would attract, but political priorities intervened. As a result, large housing estates were built before work was available for the tenants, and when the businesses which did move to Tallaght brought their workforce with them, very little new employment was created in the area. The proposed landscaping and the provision of amenities also failed to materialise.

By the mid-'80s Tallaght had become one of the worst unemployment blackspots in Ireland; indeed, in the entire European Community. In a community of 80,000 people, more than half were out of work, and in some parts of the area unemployment reached 80% of the adult population. Conversations with pastoral teams conveyed a sense of despair I had not encountered outside the most derelict inner city areas of the United States. It was difficult to reconcile this information with the Tallaght I had known many years previously, a pleasant rural village set against the backdrop of the Dublin mountains.

My first visits to this planners' Newtown left me drained and depressed. In one day alone I counted fifteen burnt-out houses. All around lay evidence of dereliction and disadvantage. The community lacked all save the most basic of services. Shops were protected with steel shuttering, fencing and iron bars as if to repel assault. Open spaces were here and there littered with burnt-out cars and rotting heaps of rubbish smouldering from recent fires; rats scurried around the waste. It took me some time to realise that these rubbish-tips were the "parkland" spaces designated on the planners' maps as green zones or amenity areas.

The people seemed impotent in their dealings with a detached, uncaring bureaucracy. The sheer waste of government funding in spurious "make-work" programmes was evident – unemployed residents who lived in conditions of near squalor were put to work tending the gardens of schools and colleges. A social programme which used placebos and not cures to avoid confronting the real problems was matched by the amateurism of well-meaning but unskilled voluntary organisations. The anger I felt at these conditions turned to red hot rage at the sight of well-guarded moneylenders holding children's allowance and pension books as security on loans, forcing their debtors to surrender the cash.

Yet there was hope, too. In the badly funded voluntary programmes for women and children, people were forging dreams of a better world. Many homes, neatly painted with tidy well kept gardens, stood like beacons in the midst of neglect. The courtesy and friendliness with which I was met in the homes I visited shone in stark contrast to their occupants' unending struggle against the twin evils of poverty and neglect.

I was convinced that the state could not provide a solution to Tallaght's problems. If the Society moved unwisely, it might be seen to assume the role of provider and it, too, would fail. But the Society, I felt, could act as a catalyst in promoting the idea of community empowerment which would give rise to a community-level response to Tallaght's problems, that is, a programme initiated and controlled by the community itself. My report for the Society was not what I had expected to write. Many of the remedies for social decay which I had seen in the Unites States were, for the present at least, inapplicable. The problems required a new approach tailored to the circumstances on the ground. Even so, there could be no guarantee of success; at best, there was only a fifty-fifty chance of making a meaningful impact on the problems of the area. The alternative, however, was to surrender to despair.

On the surface, Tallaght seemed like one area, but I felt that in fact it was made up of ten distinct communities, separated by strips of wasteland. Each had a similar identity of sorts, in part one of common adversity, but my research had shown that there were fundamental and basic differences. The error of the state agencies had been to treat Tallaght as a composite whole; in my view the best hope of community revitalisation lay in adopting a more local approach, to work with and build on this sense of identity in each area.

To start, we needed to find community leaders in each of the ten separate communities. I was convinced that the potential for such leadership existed. Many Tallaght people had been wrenched from the city centre where they had grown up, closely knit communities where families and neighbours had been important. Dispossessed as a result of urban renewal programmes and transported to an alien environment, they nonetheless brought with them a deep-seated and practical understanding of what community was all about.

The Society's task force approached a number of local people, and over several weeks debated with them our view of how the Tallaght communities might begin to tackle the problems which surrounded them. These people were well aware of the problems, but needed to be convinced that a programme of self-help could make a real impact. In most cases their doubts were overcome and they agreed to organise as a core group to initiate the project in each community. Their first step was to organise public meetings in each of these ten locations.

While the organisation of these meetings was the core groups' task, because of their relative immaturity in matters of this kind they needed a good deal of support from the Society's task force. Every adult in each parish was invited to the first meeting, which was held in schools, sports halls and churches. The objective was to discuss what response the community itself could make to the problem of unemployment. Introducing the theme, the senior member of the Society laid out his organisation's desire to help in the work of revitalising Tallaght, but also set out clearly the limits of its role: to work in support of the community's efforts, but not to lead them. The absolutely non-political nature of the community enterprise programme was emphasised. The speeches were brief and to the point. I spoke for just fifteen minutes, outlining what other communities I had worked with had done on their own account. Then I invited the audience to examine the self-help proposition in greater detail at a two-day seminar.

There was a big attendance at each of these early meetings. Many had come out of curiosity, some just to get out of the house for a few hours, and still more came with the energy and will to act. The question and answer sessions which followed the formal presentation were fast and furious as the people of the community catalogued the planning mistakes made in the area and the facilities which it lacked, and complained bitterly of how they seemed to be condemned to unemployment and a life of subsisting on social security. There were a good number of politicians from all parties present, and some officials from the state agencies, and when any tried to engage in speechifying they were ruled out of order: the focus of the meeting was on the community and what it could do, not on what the political system would one day do for it. Not surprisingly, many of the politicians were none too pleased at the low profile they were asked to adopt, although some with whom I chatted afterwards agreed totally with the non-political approach adopted.

The people were hungry for new answers, and at the end of each meeting over half the audience volunteered to participate in the community enterprise seminars. In the days and weeks that followed the notion of "self-help" was talked about and trashed out in the shops and homes and pubs of Tallaght, and in each area fully 90% of those who had signed up for the seminar turned up on the day.

The Society task force had requested that I should take on the role of course director for each seminar in all ten districts, preparing the broad text of six twenty-minute lectures each day, and working out a rota for delivery. Various members of the task force took on the job of finding suitable lecturers and worked with the local core groups to see that all the organisational details were carried out. Arrangements were made to find suitable premises, to organise tea and coffee and lunch facilities. A chairperson had to be selected for each seminar, and members of the core group briefed on how to handle the discussion groups which would follow each lecture.

None of those attending the seminar knew quite what to expect – they were starting a journey into the unknown. To focus the discussion I began by listing some examples of the way Tallaght worked as a community. In recent weeks a family which had lost its possession in a fire had been offered an immense amount of support by its neighbours; the people of one area had come together to undo the damage caused by flooding; another area had come together as a community to mourn the death of a child. Outlining the main elements of a community enterprise programme, I pointed out that this work might well appear difficult or complex, but it was generated by community spirit such as they had shown, and could not succeed without it. If Tallaght's spirit could be directed into job creation the community could not fail to benefit; the only question was to what degree.

Over the next two days the community worked through an agenda which looked at the resources Tallaght might possess, the value of supporting the local economy, the importance of small businesses, and the structures of community enterprise organisation. Sitting in small "workshop groups", issues were debated in a way which allowed each individual to develop his or her understanding of the matters under review. As the seminar drew to a close, the initiative was endorsed by all the people who attended, and an enlarged core group was elected as a committee to monitor the progress of the enterprise programme.

The months which followed the completion of the seminars was probably the most critical period of all. Follow up meetings were held in presbyteries and classrooms as task groups were briefed and their work got underway. We had decided that in the circumstances a community audit would have little relevance and that, since the Society was in the course of finding premises for the enterprise groups, a special premises group would not be necessary. Instead, the main emphasis was put on researching the skills available to Tallaght and building our understanding of the needs of the area, with a view to pinpointing how local people might begin to provide the products and services which were lacking in the community. Questionnaires were printed and prepared and the public relations group gave advance notification to all householders of the scope and extent of the questions. Teams were organised to carry out the door-to-door research.

An early response in the local needs analysis showed that many members of the community wanted to see something done about the poor state of the "parkland" spaces. The community groups negotiated with the local authority and offered to help the council undertake the work if necessary. In a very short space of time the vacant lots were cleared of rubbish and the council agreed to begin landscaping and provide playground space for children. For perhaps the very first time a sense of partnership was generated between the Tallaght community and the planning authority.

Over the next several months there were many false starts, moments of near despair, and continual frustration at the slow pace of progress. All of the groups were trying to achieve too much too quickly, but gradually they were persuaded to hasten slowly, to take one step at a time. In the event seven groups came through the first year, and grew in self-confidence and strength. Three fell by the wayside; curiously, these were situated in communities which would be regarded as the more affluent areas.

As the task groups continued with their work, it became apparent that unless a permanent headquarters was found in each community the entire programme would soon be in danger of collapse. Fortunately, a retired local government official was able to use his contacts to persuade the county council to allocate vacant premises to the community groups in four areas; in the other areas unused church or school premises were licenced to the groups. The groups begged redundant office furniture from commercial enterprises in the local industrial estates and set about furnishing their new premises.

No funding was available from the state agencies; in fact, the community groups had to work hard to achieve even the simplest objective, like securing telephone and electricity connections. FÁS did initially offer to finance the human resources and skills survey, but this offer was then withdrawn because of cutbacks in that organisation's budget. The staffing of all community offices was covered by volunteers, who handled the queries which the public brought to them, recorded and filed survey results and monitored the activities of the survey teams. They brought a sound, common-sense approach to bear on matters as they arose, and only needed professional guidance to overcome unforeseen difficulties, such as when social welfare authorities queried the unemployed status of people who spent so much time doing voluntary work for their communities.

As soon as the community headquarters were operational,

there was a surge of applications for business counselling. Initially the community groups organised these sessions as if the people coming for interview were attending a doctor's clinic, but when I found myself arriving at a community house with up to twenty people at a time awaiting interviews, I quickly realised that this would not work. An appointment system was introduced so that each person could receive adequate assessment and counselling.

In the early stages of the programme not all who came for counselling had the best motivation. Many came out of curiosity, others to claim their share of the cake, still more to demand their rights. The majority, however, had a basic idea for a business, however tentative or ill-formed. For many, this idea represented their paramount source of hope, and it was essential to thread softly to avoid trampling on their dreams. After the basic soundness of their ideas were assessed, each person was shown how to test the viability of the project by doing some basic market research; they were shown how to determine the cost of accommodation, plant or equipment, and where to find these things. Finally, once the idea was shown to be feasible and marketable, they were assisted in preparing business plans and in preparing an application for funds from state agencies or voluntary trusts. Since the majority of applicants were unemployed and could not provide collateral, they were not regarded as good risks by the commercial banks.

Not unexpectedly, many ideas foundered at the initial stages, but even in these cases the individuals involved felt that their efforts had been worthwhile. They had carried out their own research and had proved or disproved the value of their ideas for themselves. At worst, the effort they put into these projects gave them new energy to explore other options which might be open to them.

From over 1,000 counselling session in the first year, more than one hundred people succeeded in starting a business. Some people found a new outlet for the skills they had used when employed, others developed ideas from hobbies, and over the next three years their businesses showed a 75% success rate. The type and variety of start-ups covered a wide range, including machine knitwear, educational toys, glassware, upholstery, signmaking and signwriting, shopfitting, joinery, printing, security grid manufacture, computer programming, food preparation, soft toy manufacture, craft work of all kinds, curtain manufacture, specialised paint mixing. Services included sewing machine and domestic appliance repair, laundry and dry cleaning, furniture repair and reconditioning, and a whole range of building maintenance. These new self-employment ventures used the enterprise initiative's premises, which are a community resource, as a business address.

There were some real technological innovations also. When I first met Tony he had been unemployed for over four years. A handsome man in his mid-thirties, his demeanour conveyed an aura of despair when he first came for business counselling under the enterprise programme. The recession in the shipping industry gave him little hope of re-employment in his former job as shipping engineer.

Tony had a product idea for which he had tried to obtain support from a variety of state agencies, which he felt had rebuffed him with scant hearing. From his attitude it was clear he had little faith our meeting would produce a different result. Indeed, he admitted that he had come largely because the local employment exchange was insisting that he undertake a job-search programme – this would teach him how to prepare a curriculum vitae for a job. A highly-trained individual, Tony regarded this as the last straw in his unequal struggle with bureaucracy.

He opened a cardboard box which carried the results of years of patient, painstaking research, and began to explain his idea for a product to assist the disabled. His aura of despair disappeared as he described how it would work. Over the next few hours my initial curiosity turned to admiration as it became clear that he had come up with what seemed to be a dramatic technical advance. If it could be shown to be economically viable, I was convinced that Tony's innovation was vastly superior to any comparable product available.

His prototype, however unimpressive in appearance now, was an excellent example of inventive genius. Why, I wondered, had he received such a negative response from state agencies? I personally knew many of the officials to be intelligent, perceptive and compassionate. Had he failed to outline his ideas adequately? Perhaps that would explain why his concept was misunderstood and its potential unrecognised.

Today, some three years later, Tony's product is being test marketed in several countries. A number of leading US corporations have an active interest in joint venture; the EC has allocated substantial funding for research and development to widen the scope of the product's use. An idea developed in the bedroom of a West Tallaght home will bring comfort and joy to a multitude of disabled people around the world. Yet without the community enterprise programme, Tony would be yet another failed dreamer. More importantly, he is not alone. There are scores of others, people with innovative ideas, with new and different ways of doing something better, who because of the programme today walk tall. All were unemployed, either through redundancy or lack of opportunity. They felt lost, or mourned their old, comfortable occupational patterns. The enterprise programme helped them overcome their anger and frustration, and helped them see that rather than feel negative about the loss of what they knew, they had to find the courage to feel positive about what they could create. This is one of the key objectives of a successful community enterprise programme.

The unique character of the service offered under this community programme became clear when, within six months of it starting up, people were being referred to the programme by officers in the state agencies and by politicians in their constituency clinics. Yet the programme was entirely dependent on funds which the communities raised themselves, and the subvention which the Society of St Vincent de Paul provided from its own very limited resources. Even today state funding is minimal, and by and large does not extend beyond allowing the community groups to operate the social employment scheme which, in effect, replaces social welfare with an equal payment for twenty hours work on a community programme. The lack of support was felt most acutely when the groups had to undertake both the human resources and skills survey and the local needs analysis out of their own resources. As the Society's consultant to the programme I was able to give the professional assistance required in the drafting of question-naires, instruction to the groups and the volunteers from local schools who undertook the field-work, and help in the subse-quent evaluation of the surveys' results, but though the surveys were carried out effectively it was a mammoth undertaking in such a densely populated area and proved to be a real strain on the programme's energy and resources.

This lack of state support is a cause of deep resentment to many of the community groups, particularly when the positive results of the Tallaght community enterprise initiative are there for all to see. More than 400 new business start-ups are estab-lished and there are fifteen projects under active consideration each month. An enterprise centre is planned, to house new small business initiatives with the potential to grow and pro-vide them with a full range of business services. Over 1,000 adults of all ages have been helped to find full-time employ-ment, and a youth job-placement programme has been initi-ated. In the early days of the initiative, less than 10% of those employed in local businesses lived locally, but when the Square Shopping Centre opened, one of the largest complexes of its kind in Ireland, more than 50% of those recruited came from the enterprise communities' lists.

Membership of each community enterprise group is open to everyone who lives in the community. The community groups are controlled by executive committees elected annually by the members, and represent their area more fully than any other comparable organisation has ever done. Because they are part of the community, the executive members are immediately conversant with, and reactive to, the daily problems of the people and of the area. From the outset I had hoped that the individual community groups would establish close relationships with one another as they matured. This has happened and created a new dynamic, *Action Tallaght*, an association of all the surviving community groups. Because *Action Tallaght* is fully and truly representative of each community enterprise group, it derives its mandate directly from the people who live in the area, and it is in a unique position to mobilise the resources of the community. The Society of St Vincent de Paul, which initiated the community enterprise project, still plays a vital but low-key role, sourcing both professional expertise and finance to the extent that it can.

The common objective remains community revitalisation and job creation. New possibilities, new approaches, new ideas are continually opened up as the community's energy gains momentum. A whole series of programmes are underway which will lead in time to environmental improvement and to use being made of the natural scenic and leisure resources which lie in the nearby mountains. Youth programmes, and programmes to organise facilities and activities for the old, the infirm and the disabled are being organised, as are projects to encourage adult and second-chance education and affirmative action programmes to assist the most deprived within the community.

The long term goal of the association is to achieve economic self-sufficiency. The top priority is to design and implement strategies to create jobs for the residents of this disadvantaged area; it is equally important, of course, to ensure that local residents are given access to the education and training needed to hold these jobs. *Action Tallaght* adopts a comprehensive strategy which looks at the overall needs of the area, and tries to avoid the piecemeal approaches which were a feature of the past. This process entails the initiation, planning and management of innovative and holistic programmes; achieving them will depend on the dedication, co-operation and commitment of the community groups, local businesses, state bodies, labour, educational and religious organisations. The human resources are in place; what is needed are the financial resources to employ the full range of professional skills to lift these projects to a new level.

The success of the Tallaght project would be increased several hundred-fold if sufficient financial and other resources were available. By comparison with community enterprise programmes in other countries in Europe and North America, the present outcome has been achieved on a shoestring budget. The results owe much to a non-political approach and the fact that involving the community in determing it own future has generated a new sense of purpose, created a feeling of hope and sown the seeds of a new self-confidence in the community.

Community Enterprise Organisation: A Guide

Many groups have been inspired to attempt the organisation of community enterprise projects. Too many have ended in failure; others have had some success, but fallen short of the aspirations of their founders. The reasons are manifold but, in my experience, the central cause has been that the structures set up lacked one or more of the essential building blocks of community enterprise organisation. Enthusiasm is no substitute for careful step-by-step planning – mistakes made at the outset will inevitably work to stunt subsequent development.

The Tallaght experience demonstrates how much can be achieved by people with minimal financial backing, initiating a project in an area with no readily identifiable natural resources. Most places have a long tradition of community, institutions which work for the area's benefit, and natural assets which can be put to good use with a little skill and imagination. Most areas will also have problems of unemployment and emigration.

Nonetheless, it is better to light a candle than to curse the dark. In a Welsh community which faced significant redundancies when the local mine closed down, the community enterprise group approached the mine' owners and persuaded them to lease it to the locality rather than flood it as they had planned. The mine was converted into a tourist attraction and is today the centrepiece of local tourism, drawing substantial spending into the area.

Tallaght had no mine, but it did have people who were willing to assume the enormous task of finding solutions to the problems which confronted the area. The key lies in developing this community initiative in a way which makes it effective. In some cases the natural community may be too small to develop an action programme of its own, and communities such as these should find partners in the initiative. If it is to mobilise the level of skills and resources which are need to create a successful project, a sustainable community enterprise initiative will usually need to encompass a group of communities and parishes over a wide geographical area. Bonding the people into an effective partnership may require the use of a branch structure, with each local branch requiring an active membership of perhaps forty to fifty people to be self-sustaining. Its tasks would include the setting up and operation of a local centre, and each branch would liaise with and be represented in all the major activity groups.

The basic concept, structure and work of community enterprise is essentially the same, but its application will vary from place to place. The purpose, therefore, of this guide is to illustrate the laborious step-by-step approach which is required to translate the vision of a working community into reality.

Step One

First, recognise that your community repesents both a challenge and an opportunity; it is not simply a problem area to which there are no solutions. People are the community's greatest asset. No matter how richly endowed with natural resources your area may be, they are still inanimate objects. Only people can generate ideas and initiative.

There are people who have inherited disadvantages, and there are many, too, who have been treated as outcasts by our society. For them we must be prepared to reach outside tradition and precedent and construct affirmative action programmes which might include all kinds of uneconomic retraining – in literacy skills, for example, leading in time to second-chance education. The need for such programmes is identified and planned by the community, with funding sought from the relevant educational authority.

The majority, even on the margins of society, have latent abilities and skills which need to be carefully nurtured. Social research in the US revealed a higher level of entrepreneurial ability in the ghetto than in the more affluent areas, and I can confirm that much the same is true in Irish circumstances; I found more innovative ideas in Tallaght than in any other assignment I had undertaken. Given access to the necessary capital, people's own ability can provide job opportunities for people in the place where they live. The key lies in the realistic aspirations of the people in the community.

In the US Bible belt there is a saying that all effective community action involves "visualising, prayerising and actualising". So, start with your own vision of what your community can achieve. Mobilise a small group of like-minded persons to share that vision. Now you have an *ad hoc* committee to organise a meeting of the full community.

Step Two: The First Meeting

The specific purpose of this meeting is to discuss and activate a community response to unemployment. Every adult in the community should be invited. It is not advisable, at this stage, to expand the invitation list to include politicians and/or semi-state officials in their official capacity. However, if they are living in the community they have an equality of interest with all other residents.

In the past, meetings on the subject of unemployment have too often turned into an acrimonious argument between the people, state officials and politicians. Since the primary purpose of this meeting is to determine what action your community can take, divisive discussion needs to be avoided. For this reason the meeting requires a strong chairperson who can curb the possible excesses of fringe politicians or groups. A local school principal, or a leader from a women's community group, very often has the standing and local knowledge to undertake this role effectively.

The location of the meeting is a matter of judgment based on the size of the community and the attendance which is anticipated. A local school hall may have adequate facilities; very often, a local church is ideal. The Gaelic title for a church was *Teach an Phobail*, the house of the people, and it is gratifying to see it revert to its traditional role in its use for important meetings of the people.

The meeting requires one or two speakers who can generate a new sense of purpose, create new hope and sow the seeds of a new self-belief within the community. There is no prospect in one short meeting of providing all or even most of the answers: the key lies in creating the hunger for answers which will come from the detailed research and analysis which comes later. For this, the community needs to be welded together into a team, its diverse abilities pursuing a common vision and objective.

The most efficient way of starting this process is to set up a one or, preferably, two-day seminar where, through lectures and workshops, an effective programme of community research will be developed. An agreement to set up a community enterprise group and to organise such a seminar is the desired outcome of the first meeting. If that is achieved, make sure to have the names and addresses of all residents who have agreed to participate.

Step Three: A Seminar and Workshop Programme

This is the foundation stone on which a successful community enterprise programme can be built. As such, it requires careful planning and resourcing. Very often, some or all of the cost will be borne by way of sponsorship by local firms.

The seminar must cover the concept of community enterprise, the geographic and organisational framework of the community, and look at unemployment as both a challenge and opportunity. In showing how the community will work to intervene in its local economy, the seminar will demonstrate how to organise a community audit and a human resource survey, and how to undertake a local needs analysis. The legal structure of the community enterprise group should be explored. The need to find premises for the group and to organise a permanent secretariat must be discussed, as will the community's ability to mobilise financial resources. Raising and using money demands that proper accounting procedures are maintained and this, too, must be looked at. The community must also develop clear communications and good public relations.

Experience suggest that this is best covered in about twelve separate lectures over a two-day period. Maximum lecture time is about twenty-five minutes, and lectures need to be interspersed with small workshop discussions to allow for an evenness of understanding amongst all participants. Then there are coffee breaks and a lunch break each day. A final round-up decision meeting is held at the end of day two.

Retaining the service of a professional experienced in the subject matter as course director and lecturer is essential. Normally, the course director will recruit about two other speakers, so that there is a variation in voice, pace and delivery, though it is not unusual for all of the lectures to be prepared by the course director who then works out a suitable rota for delivery. Professionals with suitable experience can be found in the engineering, economics, business studies and legal faculties of third-level institutes or colleges, or in professional bodies. It is vital, however, that the lecturer addresses the subject at hand, i.e. the goals of community self-help. The purpose of the seminar is not to deliver the prevailing theory of economics or business or community politics, nor to inform the audience about state grants, training programmes or European funding. Lectures will touch on these topics, which are useful to the work of the community enterprise group, but their fundamental purpose is at all times to address the question: what can this community do to help its area develop?

Professionals with experience in community enterprise are rare in Ireland, though the debate on community initiative and empowerment has raised the profile of this issue, and universities and other institutes have responded by offering classes in community studies to the communities outside their portals. Generally, a community group will use the professional skills available, many of which may already exist in the community, but it is essential that the professionals' knowledge be bent to the subject of self-help. It is also essential to recruit the most experienced people from the community group set up at the public meeting to act as facilitators for workshop group discussions.

Choice of location for the seminar is crucial. It must be easily accessible for those wishing to attend, have an adequate auditorium or lecture hall to house the numbers comfortably, provide a sufficient number of smaller rooms for workshops of up to twelve persons, a canteen for coffee breaks and for lunch, and adequate toilet facilities. In addition, if the community has a substantial young married population, it is desirable to organise a creche for infants and young children. Normally, a local community college or school provides the best answer to these requirements, although weekends are usually the only time when these schools are available.

Before the seminar and workshop programme concludes the following require decision:

* Choosing a central or core group to assume executive control of the community enterprise initiative, to monitor the work of the group – particularly the research undertaken by the working groups – and to prepare a comprehensive business plan for the entire community enterprise programme. If a community support programme is also adopted, this requires separate planning. Generally, experience has shown that a programme of community support is put on the back burner until the enterprise group has gained confidence from establishing the enterprise programme.

* Choosing a series of small working groups (each made up

of four to six persons) who will organise the work of under-taking the community audit and human resource surveys, and the local needs analysis, which are the building blocks of the community group's intervention. Further tasks which must be carried out include, locating premises, arranging legal structuring, researching the full range of state and EC support programmes available to the community, mobilising financial resources, and organising inter-group communications and public relations.

* Organising a temporary central secretariat to provide backing to the core group and working groups.

* Setting a date, not more than one month later, for a full community meeting to receive up-dated reports from each activity group. A detailed time schedule is set out for achieving each task; progress is then measured against this critical path analysis.

* Every person who undertakes to perform a role in any of the foregoing must be required to sign a confidentiality guarantee which legally commits them to retain, in absolute confidence, all information accessed during their work on the programme. This is a legal commitment the breach of which has serious consequences. However, it is vital if the groups are to obtain the required information from members of the community at large.

The critical path analysis will set out the time schedules for achieving specific targets. Again, it is necessary to hasten slowly and to learn as you go.

Step Four: Guidance for Working Groups

Organising a Community Audit
This broad audit of the community's income and expenditure is undertaken so as to find out the degree to which local spending supports or fails to support local/regional/national jobs. Its aim is to discover where money is leaving the area unnecessarily, and seeks to identify when needs can be met lo-

cally. It deals with total community income and spending so as to build up a picture of the local economy: it is not concerned with how any one household either makes its money or spends it.

Even so the very nature of the audit creates its own difficulty. Very many people may regard responding to a comprehensive questionaire as an invasion of their privacy. This objection can be partly overcome by designing the survey so that each household's response is conveyed anonymously. It can also be argued, with some justification, that a random sample survey would provide a great deal of the basic information required. However, a key secondary objective of the survey is to focus the minds of each and every community resident on the positive or negative role which their individual everyday spending has on local, regional or national jobs. This is best achieved by a census of the entire community. Thus, this activity group should arrange the delivery of a questionnaire into every home, with an SAE to facilitate response.

The precise nature of the questionnaire will differ from community to community and will be influenced by sociological, geographic and other factors. In all cases, however, information is sought on total household income and expenditure. How much income is derived from outside the area – regionally, nationally or from abroad? How much comes from goods or service sold in or outside the area? The objective is to get the best possible estimate of total cash inflows into the community.

Expenditure will cover items such as light, power, heat, rent, purchased services, household goods, clothing and food – in fact the entire range of human needs which are bought and paid for by residents. In the case of power and fuel, the degree to which the presence or absence of adequate insulation increases or decreases the cost needs to be ascertained – this can provide both a useful business opportunity and a means of reducing the flow of money which leaves the community. The source of service and goods, in terms of point of purchase and origin, is relevant to the information required from each household.

A different questionnaire is required for local businesses. However, the objective is the same, i.e. to determine where money is leaving the community unnecessarily.

It is desirable that this group should have, as a minimum, some professional guidance in the preparation of the survey and in the analysis of results. However, a community may well find that it has these skills in the locality, in the presence of residents who work in research or marketing.

Correctly planned and implemented, this community audit can play a vital role in regaining community control over the local economy. The results can also beneficially influence inter-community support, and the exchange of goods and services between communities.

Human Resources and Skills Survey

In the past, many community groups have been persuaded to undertake this survey solely to produce statistical data and a report. This is not the objective. However interesting this result may be to state agencies or sociologists, it has very limited relevance to the planning of an effective community enterprise programme. The objective of this survey is to produce a precise, up-to-date register of the community which is subsequently used to target employment opportunities. It will indicate:

i. Those unemployed, their age, sex, skill, experience and qualification level.

ii. Those in this category who wish to explore the option of self employment.

iii. Those retired, their willingness to assist the community project and the skills they can bring to it.

iv. Those currently employed, their willingness to assist and skills level.

v. Those currently employed, anticipating redundancy, with age, sex, skills, experience and qualification level.

vi. Those self-employed, offering products or service, who by inclusion in an effective community business and services directory could expand the volume of their business and create local job opportunities.

vii. Those currently in second or third-level education, and the number of years until they will seek employment; anticipated qualifications and/or skills achievement.

All information sought during this survey must be covered by confidentiality guarantee. The information is strictly for the community register and must not be divulged to third parties without consent. Whilst every resident should be willing to supply the information required, if only from enlightened self interest, there can be no compulsion. It is important that a negative response be accepted with courtesy and good humour.

Once this survey has been completed, the community has measured its most important asset. The information gathered forms the basis for action over a number of areas:

* It identifies potential entrepreneurs for start-up businesses.

* It enables a detailed skills register to be in place as a basis for targeted job placement, negotiations with potential businesses (attracted as inward investment), and as a guide to potential training or retraining needs.

* It provides the essential briefing material for effective negotiations with state, semi-state and EC agencies.

* It provided the basis for a realistic search for innovation and technology transfer.

Depending on the size of the community, the time and resources required to undertake this survey can be formidable. Professional help in the design, supervision and interpretation of the survey is desirable, though not essential if sufficient initial basic training is provided during and immediately following the seminar.

In the past, communities have received assistance from local businesses in the design and printing of the questionnaire and in the provision of computer facilities for processing the response. The people required for the heavy volume of field work have in many instances come from senior students of local second-level or third-level colleges. In other cases, a suitable social employment scheme has provided the necessary number of persons required. However recruited, all field workers require basic training and hands-on supervision. Additionally, it is essential for adequate insurance cover to be in place throughout the survey. The human resources and skills working group must determine the most appropriate way of going about this work. However, the satisfactory conclusion of the work is crucial to the effective development of the community.

Local Needs Analysis

This is the area which causes most difficulty for community groups. The reason may be the catch-all nature of the brief and the inability of the group to see how a business opportunity can be developed from an apparently simple idea. The object of the analysis is to look around at the needs of the community, and see how local people or firms can meet these needs by providing goods or services.

For a local needs analysis in most communities, the most fruitful starting point is for each group member to organise a series of informal discussions held at random locations over the target area. Small discussion groups are best; a maximum number of ten to twelve people is a good rule. A cup of tea or coffee helps to ensure informality. The working group members act as facilitators, encouraging an active discussion on what the group sees as community needs, and avoid promoting their own pet ideas. All ideas and information which comes out of the discussion are noted.

In an area in Northern Ireland where a community group was looking at local needs, a considerable number of people spoke of their frustration in trying to clean domestic ovens. A young unemployed man latched on to the idea. His researched the best methods of cleaning ovens and then set up his own "oven cleaning round". Simple though the initial idea may have been, his enterprise has grown to a business with a six-figure turnover, employing five people:

In a similar example from the USA, another young unemployed man got his idea as he watched the underside of a pleasure boat being cleaned with a stand-alone pressure pump. He thought of the number of complaints he had overheard concerning the difficulty of cleaning oil and grass from shopping forecourts and domestic driveways. Matching this information to the tools (or, if you like, technology) which were available, he hired the pressure-pump equipment and set about providing a fast, efficient cleaning service. Today he employs thirty people, cleaning buildings, walls, industrial and shopping forecourts and domestic driveways.

It is all a case of meeting social needs at a profit. So let us commence with the basic concept that no idea is too simple to warrant consideration as a potential business opportunity.

As well as organising group discussion, a structured random sample research within the target area can also be productive. However, in my experience, most groups have found the result disappointing, probably because they lacked the technical expertise of professional market research organisations. In addition, it is well to be mindful that the two activity groups previously discussed are already in the field drawing on people's time.

Product and service ideas, compatible with your community needs, can very often be discovered from research with the Irish Goods Council, the IDA's Products Division and the advertising pages of foreign newspapers and magazines. Other sources are the regular newsletter of foreign embassies' trade sections, US and UK enterprise agencies, newspapers and EC small business magazines. Local people now living abroad, can be recruited as useful sources of intelligence, including obtaining directories of franchise organisations in foreign countries.

Next comes research with existing businesses within the target area to determine potential for growth from the use of ideas sourced.

When the community enterprise group has reached a stage of development which allows it access to innovative venture and technology transfer, this mechanism, too, can provide local existing business with excellent expansion opportunities.

Close co-operation with, and a detailed study of, the results emerging from the human resources and skills survey is essential. This identifies potential entrepreneurs with business ideas, suitable candidates for entrepreneurial training and matching to compatible business ideas.

If this group approaches its tasks with an open, enquiring mind, free from prejudice, and avoids hasty judgment, it will significantly contribute to the community's revitalisation.

Premises

This is a specialist group with three central tasks. The first is to identify and acquire an immediate, if temporary, base for the community enterprise programme. A group without a central operating office is handicapped from the very start; its lack can cause premature failure of the community effort. Ideally, the premises acquired should be sufficient to house all the activity groups and be equipped to facilitate their smooth operation. Adequate security for confidential papers is essential, as is the arranging of adequate insurance cover.

Communities have met this first need in a variety of ways. In some areas, unused or under-utilised church or school premise were made available. In others, local authorities allocated premises for community use. Occasionally, private property owners were willing to licence the use of vacant premises, although this was occasionally frustrated by the loss of rates relief. Clearly each community must seek it own solution from the properties available in the area.

The next task of the premises group is to determine, in conjunction with the other working groups, whether a centralised enterprise centre is required or whether, in say a widely spread rural community, a core centre with one or more satellite units is preferable. Much depends on what best suits the needs of the community. An enterprise centre is only justified when there are sufficient small businesses looking for premises to make the provision of a centre viable. If a decision is taken to establish an enterprise centre, suitable premises must be found. Great care needs to be exercised in the choice of premises to minimise conversion and/or repair costs. It is also important to ensure that sub-letting through licences is not legally excluded.

The premises group will be responsible for the task of getting the premises up to the required standards for its projected use. This will require liaison with the planning authority, the local fire officer and familiarisation with departmental regulations. Thereafter, the premises must be furnished to the required standards with full provision of telephone, fax, power and light, security systems etc. In the medium to long term, this group will assume the role of property managers for the community enterprise group.

Legal Structuring of the Community Enterprise Group

Again, this is a specialist group which usually comprises lawyers and accountants who are resident in the community. However, unlike the premises group, this is an activity of limited duration.

In Britain and Ireland, the structure for the community enterprise group is usually either the Co-Operative (or Friendly) Society or a Company Limited by Guarantee. Although I personally favour the second choice, it is really a matter of individual judgment. Since lawyers and accountants have both knowledge and experience of these structures, it is unnecessary to develop here the implications of the choice made; both forms have an equally strong basis to encompass community enterprise objectives. Regretably, I have experienced many instances where unintentional ommissions from the objective clauses have caused difficulties to communities at the later stages of development. Sometimes this can arise because of confusion as to the future activity of the community enterprise as it develops and matures. For this reason, it is best to outline the objectives which, in addition to the general objects usually incorporated, could beneficially be incorporated into the rules or memorandum of registration, whichever legal format is adopted. Accordingly, the objects of the Society (or Company) shall be:

To undertake and perform all acts or deeds which the Society (Company) may legally undertake and perform which, in the opinion of the Management Committee (or Directors), will benefit the community of "X" and, specifically, but without prejudice to the generality of the foregoing:

i. To make donations or subscriptions to any society, institution, trust, organisation or charity now existing or hereafter to exist for the general purpose of all or any of the following objectives – community revitalisation, the relief of poverty, the generation of employment, the provision of education and/or training in skills or otherwise for the betterment of individuals or communities.

ii. To establish and promote an enterprise centre, community support centres, craft centres, business and technology centres or workspace centres to encourage young people, unemployed persons and others to establish their own businesses and to assist small business enterprise.

iii. Contains the usual general clauses which give the Society (Company) the authority to acquire lands, property etc. and powers to borrow monies in order to promote the objects of the Society (Company).

iv. Empowers the Society (Company) to hire or supply labour for the carrying out of any work.

v. Provides that the Society (Company) may advance or lend any of the capital or other monies of the Society (Company) for the time being with or without security to persons, groups, societies or other organisations establishing businesses which in the opinion of the Management Committee (Directors) can generate employment or other benefits to the community.

vi. Empowers the Society (Company) to invest in and to take part in the management, supervision or control of business enterprises established for the benefit of communities and for that purpose to appoint and remunerate any directors, accountants, solicitors, business consultants or other experts or agents.

vii. To establish fundraising campaigns and/or promote, encourage and accept donations from any suitable source either in Ireland or elsewhere to provide funding which shall be applied to the objects of the Society (Company).

viii. To promote surveys and studies to identify skills levels within communities and to identify and negotiate the transfer of compatible innovations or technologies which can generate employment within communities upon such terms and conditions as the Management Committee (Directors) in their absolute discretion may decide.

ix. Generally to engage in any business or transaction which may seem to the Management Committee (Directors) directly or indirectly conducive to the promotion of employment or community revitalisation.

x. To do all such things consistent with the laws governing the activities of Societies (Companies) as may to the Management Committee (Directors) in their uncontrolled discretion appear to be incidental or conducive to the purpose aforesaid or any of them.

The inclusion of these objectives should permit the Community Enterprise Society or Company to adopt and implement the most extensive of community revitalisation and job creation programmes.

Secretariat

A central secretariat has the task of co-ordinating and supervising the many activities of the community enterprise group. Ultimately, and in the shortest space of time, it will be the nucleus for the management of the entire community programme.

Initially, it ensures that each activity group prepares and submits a detailed timed schedule for undertaking and completing its tasks. The secretariat will ensure that each activity group has and maintains adequate resourcing to achieve its objective, and tracks the progress of their work.

A secondary task of the secretariat is the organisation of security, e.g. authorisation for and the briefing of all persons calling on houses in the community, setting the limits of representation and the standards to be observed. Nothing should be left to chance. There have been too many instances of unscrupulous individuals fraudulently collecting monies from the public in the name of communities. Also the public image of the community enterprise group can be damaged by any wrongful act of any of its members purporting to represent the community, whether committed inadvertantly or deliberately. The public should be actively encouraged to telephone the secretariat for confirmation of authority; local gardaí should be informed of field-work taking place and the identity of the community field-workers. It takes only one or two careless incidents to destroy the most professionally organised public relations programme.

The office of the secretariat will need to be open and competently manned during all of the hours when activity groups are engaged in field-work. This, in the early months, will require shift work operations and a programmed manning schedule. Staffing by just one person alone, either day or night, must be discouraged for security reasons.

The office of the secretariat will require secure cabinets, adequate furnishing, lighting and heating, telephone, fax, a photocopier, a word processor and all other normal office requisites. However voluntary, it must exude a totally professional ambience.

Financial Resources Group
One of the most frequent of misjudgments of voluntary community enterprise groups is to regard this activity as that of a

fund-raising committee. Its primary role is much larger and of major significance to the successful establishment and operation of the entire programme. Of course, like all other activity groups, its members must assist in raising the seed funding for the initial activities of the group. However, the financial group's essential task is to determine the precise budget which will be needed to implement the overall enterprise strategy which the group adopts. It must liaise with all other groups and anticipate needs with accurately assessed cash-flow projections.

It is unlikely that any community will be in a position to raise, from its own resources, the whole or even the substantial part of the funding it requires. It is, however, essential that the community contributes to the extent that it can: a community unwilling to invest in its own development has no future. Consequently, all possible sources of community funding must be reviewed. Included will be direct solicitation of funds from key businesses or private investors, who will be asked to give planned-giving investment over a three-year period; the organisation of non-stop draws, social functions and other events.

There is a wide variety of state, local government and European programmes which can be used to leverage community funding. Some provide or pay for service or personnel costs, which reduces the burden on the community's own resources. Others directly grant-aid specific initiatives. There are a number of philanthrophic trusts and organisations which give grants or soft loans in specific circumstances. Finally, there is the PESP programme as detailed in a previous chapter of this book. All are sources which need exploring.

Central government funding includes direct grant aid from state departments which cover, amongst other things, recycling projects, community development, voluntary service to the deprived, and women's self-help groups. Some local authorities provide grants in CODAN areas – areas of extreme disadvantage – for certain capital and development expenditures. The Commission of the European Communities has published an excellent guide to grants and loans from the EC; FÁS and the IDA publish a wide range of literature on their programmes which requires study. However, caution is needed. Very many programmes are underfunded and are subject to suspension without warning. This is one area where you do not count upon any receipts until you have a commitment in writing. Every community must keep its finger on the pulse of subvention programmes which may be beneficial in leveraging the community's own funding. Be aware, however, that the rhetoric does not always fit the reality!

To the financial resources group also falls the task of devising and introducing accounting procedures and financial controls. Where the funds of the community are concerned, things must not alone be right, they must be watertight. There must be no room for doubt; nothing can damage a community more than the suspicion of malfeasance. The application of tight financial control procedures is not just desirable, it is essential.

Communications and Public Relations

The function of this activity group is to organise the flow of communication within the community enterprise group and between the group and the community. Its work includes:

* Information flow between working groups.
* Information to the broader community.
* Liaison and co-operation with other national and international community groups.
* Information releases to the general public and media.
* Determining the best methods of obtaining accurate feedback of the general community response. This is essential if the community ethos of the project is to be maintained.

Methods of communications are, at all times, a matter of best judgement. They will probably include the use of a community newsletter, church porch/pulpit publicity, public relations releases to local and national press and radio, and to television. This group should always be alert to human interest stories which can focus favourable attention on the community initiative.

More than any other, this group will determine the public perception of the entire community programme. To fulfil its function it must keep itself fully informed of developments within all of the community activity groups. It must be an authoritative source of information on the overall community enterprise strategy and how it is being implemented.

These tasks present a formidable challenge, and demand a great deal of discipline, dedication and effort from every sector of the community. Yet work of equal difficulty has been undertaken in many other spheres of life. Many of our institutions – the agricultural co-operative societies, trade unions, women's associations, sports and cultural organisations – were and are built on co-operative community endeavour. In the same light, we can build a solid economic foundation in our communities. If enough communities accept the challenge we will mine the full potential of our people, and help ensure that national policies are framed to complement the work of community enterprise initiative.

The Modern Enterprise Community

SOME YEARS AGO I was part of a delegation seeking support from the Minister for Industry and Commerce for a community enterprise development in Dublin. As we began to explain the concept, the minister remarked that he knew all about community enterprise; he had an enterprise project, he said, in his own constituency. I discovered later that he was referring to a drop-in centre for the unemployed.

Yet the minister had just a few weeks previously received a report from the National, Economic and Social Council on the Liege community enterprise project, which had been introduced and funded by the European Community. As a result of this experiment the Commission had recommended that member states should consider the implementation of similar enterprise programmes in their communities.

Government ministers, and others charged with developing our economic policies, need to look again at the potential of community enterprise. In particular, they should examine the employment-creating possibilities which are latent in community-based initiatives and set about implementing the legislation which can assist local groups to develop full-scale enterprise communities.

The simple concept of community enterprise is not new – people have always found the need for co-operative community effort in order to survive and develop. The modern enterprise community, however, was born in the United States during the recession of the 1960s and '70s, as an instrument for job creation through new business development. It started with the recognition that the foundations for the wealth of modern US business were laid during the depression of the

1920s. Over 60% of the *US Fortune 500* list has grown from ventures started back then by people with ideas like Alexander Graham Bell, Henry Ford and Tom Watson. In the 1920s these people with inventions and innovations, with different ways of doing something better, worked for long hours alone in dark garages and old basements. They became North America's entrepreneurs, providing goods and services, creating jobs, building companies that grew and made the free enterprise system work.

Any study of the 1920s will show that today's *Fortune 500* were not always so fortunate. Some never made it and their ideas were subsequently acquired by others. For every original company that grew big, there were hundreds of smaller ones quietly successful. Through hard work, good ideas, a little luck and a lot of support, they succeeded in bringing their innovations and inventions to the marketplace. Irish examples of equivalent developments are W. & R. Jacob, which started as two brothers baking biscuits for supply to ships and expanded to become an internationally known biscuit manufacturing company; Waterford Glass, which was started by the McGrath and Griffin family as the re-birth of a traditional Waterford craft industry, and the Munster & Leinster Bank and the National Bank (now both part of Allied Irish Banks) which started from humble beginnings to achieve national and indeed international status.

William C. Norris was one such businessman and, as founder and former chairman of the Control Data Corporation, was proud of the fact that he had clawed his way to the top during the 1920s and '30s as an entrepreneur. He had empathy with the lonely innovator and even in the prosperous 1950s condemned the "shrine of big business" in a lecture at Harvard University. Norris wanted to provide entrepreneurs and small businesses, both service and manufacturing, with the same facilities and support that large corporations enjoyed, without taking away their independence. He planned to provide job opportunities and a good working environment for depressed communities and, above all, to provide a technology centre in which inventive ideas and individual initiative could grow. Technology centres were founded to provide just such support for fledgling business. And they proved successful: where the initial concept was adhered to, failure rates were reduced from 90% to 10% and wealth and job creation ensued. These successes were not confined to an educated middle class: very many inventors and innovators were from the black ghettos, some of whom could neither read nor write. A black inventor who designed a small welding gun which revolutionised production lines and repair methods throughout the US, signed his first licencing agreement with an X.

New expressions and words evolved in the US to describe the modern evolution of community enterprise and to denote specific kinds of approaches to supporting new business development. Thus the terms business and technology, business innovation centre and enterprise centre describe separate developments of the same concept, with differing emphasis on its specific aspects. These terms have been borrowed in the UK and Ireland to describe very inadequate imitations of the original, and are used to cover everything from workspace developments to job creation programmes and advice centres.

As business and technology centres developed and flourished in the US, very many of the leading third-level institutes found they were losing some of their most promising talent to these centres. They introduced an "on campus" variation of the theme under the title of innovation centres. These had measurable but limited success. The sponsoring industries reported poor returns on investment over a five-year period, and complained that academics were more interested in technical excellence than profitability in the marketplace. The enterprise centre terminology came into use to describe the expansion of the technology centre concept to incorporate extensive social and community renewal, in addition to wealth and job creation projects.

The majority of these models do not adhere strictly to a

given definition, because there is no universal panacea which can be applied to cover all the circumstances found in an area or community. Adaptations which draw on all models for inspiration are common. There is, however, one constant factor. This is the provision, at a cost affordable to all participants, of resource support, seed and venture capital funding and an effective system of innovative business and technology transfer.

This demand for support for small business grew louder during the recession of the 1970s, and as a result of this recession the real importance of small business in terms of secure employment came to be acknowledged. Central to the US initiative, too, was the recognition that the 1980s and '90s would prove to be a significant era for US industry and the growth of small business. As high technology industries such as electronics, telecommunications, data processing, energy and the biological sciences were beginning to burgeon and the service sector, including health care, advertising, banking, television, videos, etc. was growing to meet international demands, new business start-ups would flourish. Many would make the *Fortune 500* list of the year 2000, but not without support that would dramatically reduce the average 90% failure rate of new business ventures.

As these centres developed and flourished in the US certain key factors emerged from their experience:

* Despite technological changes which have dramatically affected employment patterns, long-term or permanent unemployment is neither inevitable nor economically justified. Wealth creation and job creation stem from meeting society's unmet needs at a profit, and many needs still exist.

* Entrepreneurship is not a purely creative development. With very rare exceptions, entrepreneurs get at least the germ of their ideas from someone else. As well as that, most innovators and inventors, whilst anxious to make money, do not relish the thought of corporate responsibility. So why not transfer ideas from centre to centre on a royalty basis? This, after all, is how the whole practice of licencing and franchis-

ing began, and the use of these basic ideas is capable of being widely expanded.

* Innovative thinking is demanded and is available, but very often it is stymied by the failure of the state and other institutions to accept the institutional independence which the innovator requires and, indeed, creates. There is an excessive mortality rate for new or radical concepts, even when they may answer the pressing needs of society.

* By and large, big business has lost the ability to foster real innovation. Research and development budgets are absorbed in making cosmetic improvements to existing products. On the other hand, a vast amount of worthwhile innovations and technical advances gather dust in the research archives of big business.

* Innovation is best described as "defining a need, conceiving an idea, inventing a solution and then using it". In other words, business formation is the key goal, and this is true whether it takes the form of a product or service. The test of that innovation is the vote of the marketplace. Without market demand, innovation cannot have commercial success and cannot contribute to either wealth or job creation.

* Apart from areas such as art, there is no such thing as a finished product; that is, something purchased for itself. A product is a contract for the delivery of a future service. Food may be bought on appearance but it is purchased in expectation of taste; a quarter-inch drill is the expectation of a quarter-inch hole. It is this service content of the product which is most important in either marketing or effective licensing of production.

These are key principles which any business-minded person will readily understand, and indeed there is nothing very complex about them. In sum, if you require an idea to start or expand a business, you can, most probably, acquire the idea on a fee and royalty basis from its inventor, whether it originates in the US, the UK or elsewhere. If enterprise communities find that good ideas are being blocked by uneccessary restrictions or red tape, they can use the community's strength to negotiate a compromise. Good ideas are available to small local businesses: it is a fallacy to think that if an idea is worthwhile it will be grabbed by big business. Nonetheless, you can have the best idea since sliced bread but if people won't buy it you are wasting your time and money. At the end of the day, customer satisfaction is the key to successful business and secure employment.

In previous chapters we have discussed what a community can do to support employment creation on its own initiative and with a minimum of professional help. Even on a shoestring budget, which can be raised in the locality, the results will not be inconsiderable, as is shown by the Tallaght programme. In many rural and urban areas the establishment of fifteen to twenty small businesses and the placement of fifty or sixty people in employment will benefit the locality to an appreciable extent, and communities can achieve a multiple of ten, twenty or thirty times that figure even when they operate on their own initiative. However, if we are to turn the critical unemployment situation around, much more is required. I have no doubt that it can be done, but it calls for action beyond the single community area, on a regional and national level.

The community enterprise strategy which has had such a marked effect in the USA, and which has come to be recognised more and more in the European Community, is built on a number of factors. These factors, which will ensure a several hundred-fold increase in the results which can be won by single communities, are discussed here; each of the elements are looked on as being of equal weight and importance. The effective organisation and implementation of these measures demands an input from communities, acting individually and co-operating with other communities on a regional or national basis. It demands also the input of professional and industrial groups which can provide business expertise, from financial institutions, from employers' and workers' organisations and, not least, the input of central government, which must provide

both financial incentives and enabling policies which will promote these vital measures.

The Expertise Required

The creation of jobs and the development of local economies is
dependent on fostering the entrepreneur. The word "entrepreneur" conveys very different meanings to different people.
Personally, I liken entrepreneurship to the parable in the gospel
which speaks of the kingdom of heaven as analogous to the
man who discovers a pearl of great price buried in a field. He
hides the pearl, sells all he possesses, and buys the field. The
true entrepreneur is a person with a business idea who is prepared to gamble all that he possesses in order to achieve his
ambition. Believe me, they are a rare breed.

Yet, generally, he is a lonely and often frightened specialist
who is suspicious of those who offer him assistance. He is often
unclear about or unaware of the possible assistance available,
or confused by the multiplicity of offers made to him, and instead ploughs ahead on his own. He is usually undercapi-
talised, financially ignorant and familiar with only a limited
number of management functions. His strength is his qualification in his own speciality. When he decides to go into business
he is suddenly vulnerable, and this vulnerability is heightened
by the need to divert his attention to unproductive day-to-day
administrative activities. As a result, most potential entrepreneurs never succed in creating actual businesses, and if they
do, the likelihood of failure is 80% or higher.

This problem is not unique to Ireland: it has its mirror image
in virtually every western economy. The Irish semi-state support agencies have tried to answer these problems with programmes such as "Start Your Own Business" training courses
or the provision of occasional monitoring by executives from
big business. Regretably, I have seen no evidence that these
measures have impacted on the problems to any large extent
or answered individual needs in these areas. In the US and the
UK, however, I have encountered very many different ap-

proaches which have successfully tackled these issues and reduced the failure rates of new businesses to about 10% of
start-ups. Generally, this has been achieved by setting up consultative resource companies which provide services to municipalities, development authorities, local enterprise groups and
individual entrepreneurs either on a fee basis or by way of equity participation in developments. All of these companies have
the following critical elements and resources:

* Availability of trained, experienced professional staff.
* A private enterprise approach.
* An effective methodology for identifying potential entre-
preneurs or growth businesses including thorough selection
screening.
* Access to seed and venture capital funds.
* Experience in exploiting funds to the maximum possible
degree using all possible aids.
* Support systems for entrepreneurs all through their growth
pattern.
* A thorough knowledge of and the ability to plan the physi-
cal environment required to develop small business.
* Access to, and support from, institutes of learning.
* The capacity to involve local communities at all levels in en-
terprise activities.
*A sophisticated approach to innovative business and tech-
nology transfer.

We have the range of expertise required for such resource
companies; the suitable professional staff exist in third level institutes, industry, banking and in private practice. However,
any attempts which have been made to set up such resource
companies in Ireland have foundered. This arises primarily from
the common perception of the state as the grand provider; as
a result of this attitude there is a deep reluctance to pay money
for services which "the state ought to be providing". Banks
and other institutions fear that if they put in place effective resource units, the service will be expected on a charitable basis
and they will be seen to replace the state in this role. Yet the

success of the local community enterprise group will mirror the success of the small businesses developed by entrepreneurs. These are, usually, people who previously held a company job with a structured working life. Once they become businesspeople, however, their life ceases to have that structure. From the very start they face choices that are wide and full of pitfalls and, all too often, they have neither the time, expertise nor sheer resources of energy to cope. The entrepreneur, therefore, needs a business advisor, a champion who knows a great deal about organisation, operations, planning, marketing and financing. In no country in the western world have I seen official state agencies with the resources and ability to fulfil this function.

Financial institutions and individuals will only invest money in seedling businesses provided a return can be reasonably assured. Given the normal profile of the entrepreneur, this can usually only happen through continued monitoring of the young business by a qualified professional so as to ensure that the potential exhibited by the entrepreneurial ideas reach fruition. Their assistance is vital if community enterprise groups are to establish working relationships and communications with similar groups and centres in the UK; only then can Irish communities and enterprise centres become part of a network for technology transfer, with the development of appropriate exchanges of information, talents, products and services. Local enterprise groups and community co-operatives also require the availability of this kind of expertise which, in other countries, is provided by consultative resource companies. The professional ability available through consultative resource companies becomes the catalyst which ensures that local development plans, enterprise centres and the ideas of the entrepreneurs and small businesses, married to the correct financial strategy, give rise to contagious growth. This growth creates jobs.

As a nation and as a people we need a fundamental change in our own attitudes. We need to abandon our huckster approach to life and realise the false economy of amateurism. If we are sick we go to a qualified doctor; if our animals are ill we call the veterinarian. If jobs are to be created our local economies need a massive uplift in creative, productive activity. Surely, when our local economies are dying and our children are facing a bleak future, we must have the sense to seek help. If the effort/reward ratio is right, the qualified professionals are available to assist our development.

Financing Development

Webster's Dictionary defines venture as "an undertaking involving chance, risk or danger, especially a speculative business enterprise". Venture capital is the money made available for investment in such an enterprise.

In the following paragraphs we discuss how business ventures can be funded. Here, again, single communities or even groups of communities face a difficulty. A certain amount of capital can be raised in most localities for a small-scale fund which is used to support self-employment ventures, the formation of a co-operative group or to help develop a small business idea, and this can be filled out using the financial support which is available for employment- or business-related initiatives from state or European funding. Valuable though this fund undoubtedly is locally, in a national context the scale of business development which is required can only be met by a national venture capital fund. The Culliton Report, too, underlines the need for venture capital to be made available to small businesses. If the Irish banks are to be persuaded to take an active role in this regard, it will require significant change in current legislation to allow them to do so; it will also require a sea-change in current thinking. It may well be the case that government will need to offer financial incentives and perhaps some form of state guarantee to venture companies before the institutions which hold money in Ireland will be willing to put it to work in the high-risk area of providing venture capital.

In business terms, a venture is a young company or a group

of individual entrepreneurs seeking equity capital from outside the company or group. It might be a start-up enterprise or it may be a going concern in its early stages which has raised some initial capital and now seeks second or even third stage funding. In the western world this type of capital is usually obtained through private financing or a public underwriting. Most new enterprises obtain their early capital needs from private sources; however, when the stock market is enjoying a "bull" period for new issues, underwriting of start-up, speculative ventures are possible. Oil and mineral exploration are the most obvious examples.

Venture capital is sought by a new or growing company to enable it to develop and carry forward its business plan, generally with an eye to the prospect of going public in the future. The capital is usually provided by sophisticated investors seeking speculative investments which offer potentially substantial capital gains. The search by the entrepreneur for such capital can be time-consuming, expensive and frustrating. Experts with backgrounds in raising money are usually only interested in propositions which can carry adequate rewards for their services.

In the 1960s and '70s there was a very ample supply of venture capital available in the US and many billions of dollars were invested in talented people with good business ideas. These decades saw the growth of private and public venture capital funds such as the Small Business Investment Corporations and private partnerships. Lawyers, accountants, bankers and professional "finders" thrived on the harvest. The financial pages of daily newspapers, popular financial magazines and journals carried announcements advertising new financings and these were a productive source for entrepreneurs looking to access capital. Today, however, the market throughout the western world has contracted.

An investor is attracted to venture capital funding by a high return on investment. He recognises that he is exposed to a high risk situation and, in consequence, expects the returns to be high. This is known as the "risk-reward" ratio which can vary from a return of five to twenty times or more. To be attractive to a venture capital investor, a young company or start-up enterprise must demonstrate the ability to provide experienced, talented management, a product or service with a large potential market, patent protection, skilled know-how, the willingness to work towards public flotation, a company profile which is likely to have an above-average price/earnings ratio and an initial valuation of equity which is reasonable.

Regrettably, in Ireland we have never had true venture capital companies. Those that have been established, usually with fairly substantial banking investment, have set minimum levels of turnover and market achievement which most businesses can only achieve after a considerable number of years. They also set relatively large minimum sums, usually no less than £200,000, which is generally of no use to the individual starting off in a small way. This has left Irish entrepreneurs and small business dependent on bank borrowing, lease purchasing and hire purchase to finance start up and initial growth. Seed and venture capital is not generally available and borrowing is subject to the provision of adequate security. There is an indisputable need for small and medium-sized businesses to have easier access to capital for both start-ups and early expansion. The position in Ireland compares very unfavourably with that in other countries, like Germany, where a more active role is played by the banking institutions.

In fairness to the Irish banks, it must be said that they are constrained by the very tight legal regulations and licensing conditions imposed by the Central Bank under the laws of the Republic. These laws and regulations also severely restrict the establishment of schemes by local groups to set up investment funds or to fund soft loans to small entrepreneurs. Whilst the laws are probably necessary to protect depositors from fraud or rash investment, it is surely within the capacity of our lawmakers to provide certain exemptions in order to assist *bona fide* community enterprise development. One such amendment would have assisted a Dublin community group which was forced to abandon plans for investment by local people because the scheme offended banking laws.

This has been a factor in limiting Irish entrepreneurial development and has been a primary reason for small businesses failing, or failing to grow. If we are to make a meaningful impact on current unemployment figures here in Ireland, this position needs urgent remedy. We might look once more at an Israeli example. The State of Israel achieved economic miracles with the finance gained from Jewish communities throughout the world when it invited subscription to Israeli state bonds, with the funds being invested in development projects in Israel. A bond issue backed by the state for venture capital investment in the development of Irish entrepreneurial activity would, in my view, raise considerable capital for investment. Subscriptions to such an issue could be sought both in Ireland and from the Irish abroad. Local enterprise groups could target their own seed and venture capital funding which could then be leveraged from a national venture capital funding agency, providing grants and loans.

The extensive use of Municipal Bond issues in the US to fund municipally-led revitalisation programmes provides an example of local-level funding which, with some adaptation and generous tax concessions, could yield a worthwhile harvest for local community development. In the USA municipalities have the right to raise money by way of bond issues for municipal development of all kinds; there is no reason why county councils here could not do the same if they were given the legislative authority to do so. The rewards to both bond holders and local fund subscribers would need to be attractive. These rewards would derive from the success of investment in new and growing businesses. Returns would come from either dividends, takeouts at higher valuations by entrepreneurs, sale of stock to other investors or public issues. The risk involved demands a substantial risk/reward ratio. In other countries medium risks have carried multiples of four to seven and high risks multiples of eight to ten or more over a four to seven year period.

Capital raised in this fashion coupled with an enterprise programme which contains the key elements previously described,
could and would be a powerful antidote to the cancer of unemployment. Big ideas and small business go hand in hand
but usually have more creativity than money. Properly capi-
talised, they have proven to be the most secure area for business and job development – in very many areas of the USA
87% of all new jobs originate in small business.

The Vital Missing Ingredient

The vital missing ingredient in virtually all United Kingdom and
Irish community developments is an effective system of innovative venture and technology transfer.

Before defining and discussing this in detail, it is essential to
be clear on the commercial facts of life. In subsequent paragraphs I discuss in some detail the millions of innovations
which are held in databanks by several American corporations
who act as agents for the patent or copyright owner, licencing
or franchising the owner's idea to third parties. None of these
are philantrophic bodies. In virtually all cases the databank is
jealously guarded and access is granted to subsidiary or associate consultancies for substantial fees. These consultancies, in
turn, use this privilege as a vital element in negotiating highly
rewarding consulting assignments for area revitalisation and
job creation which they obtain from, amongst others, municipalities or local authorities, private enterprise industrial park
developments, large companies seeking new product ideas,
and so on.

A community enterprise group, a single company, or a charitable trust cannot expect to gain access to this system; in fact,
having worked in this area in the USA, I am aware of no instance where access was granted to governments or their
agencies. Yet accessing this programme is vital if we are to ac-
celerate the generation of ideas which can provide the basis for
existing businesses to expand or new businesses to start, both

of which are necessary to increase employment. In Ireland this can be done by setting up a private company with substantial funds at regional or, more probably, national level. In turn this company can pay the high entry fee that is required to join the system, and, because of its financial strength, can covenant to adhere to the strict confidentiality terms which are applied and to guarantee payment of future royalties to the licencee.

But what exactly is innovative venture and technology transfer? Very simply, when an individual or group in the USA developed a new concept for a service or manufacturing business in their home state, let's say Maryland, they were in most cases content to trade in that state. Even when they grew, they were still happy to stay in the environment that they knew best. Yet their ideas had potential in other states with compatible environmental and market factors. So, as part of community job creation programmes in the USA, the Maryland group were approached by upwards of thirty other locations in the USA to franchise or licence their idea for a different market. The inventor got royalties from expanded sales and the new location got jobs. When one realises that there are over five million such situations as the Maryland example, it is not surprising that computerising and transferring these innovations became a business in itself.

In a policy document issued as far back as 1984, the Directorate General of the European Commission set out guidelines for enterprise development which acknowledged that innovative venture and technology transfer enhanced the chances of success of individual community schemes and projects considerably. In this, the Directorate echoed the view of many major European firms, like Olivetti, British Steel, Shell, F.N. de Herstal and Prudential, who wanted to contribute to the creation of new small businesses, both for reasons of social responsibility and as investment opportunities. Central to the thinking of both groups was the fact that innovative venture and technology transfer created growing job opportunities, particularly suited to depressed urban areas. This type of transfer has been demonstrated time and time again both to inject a new dynamic into existing businesses and to form a secure basis for new business formation.

Little appears to cause greater difficulty with our semi-state agencies here in Ireland than this concept of innovative venture and technology transfer. They argue that the banks and other agencies are already engaged in transferring whatever suitable technology exists and that if it were possible to mount transfer on a larger scale it would have already been done. Of course, the state agencies have always been alert to sourcing new concepts; after all, this is a job for experts. Such is the accepted wisdom of the state.

It is true that the state agencies, both in Ireland and the UK have made probes into the area of acquiring technology transfer, but their efforts have had little success for three principal reasons. They were unaware of precisely what they were seeking and where to find it; they had inadequate data as to the skills and compatible market circumstances which they were trying to match; and they failed to overcome the deep-seated suspicion most innovative entrepreneurs, especially in the USA, have towards state bodies.

The central difficulty of sourcing innovations and technologies, required as the basis for new business development and job creation, emerged as the major limiting factor also in early programmes in the United States. Some proposals put forward by entrepreneurs were sufficiently advanced to permit a rapid development of the product or service and only needed backing; the majority, however, were in the embryonic stage, untested and unproven. It was found that many more innovative ideas were needed if a meaningful impact was to be made on community revitalisation, wealth creation and job creation. It was thought that these problems might be answered by transferring technology through franchising and/or licensing, but research quickly showed that this solution had a major limitation – technology was perceived by governments and big business purely in terms of high technology. There was also an absence of an effective and relatively inexpensive mechanism for transfer: only a few high-tech products with considerable market potential were economic given the expense of traditional one-to-one transfer. And, regrettably, such transfers rarely created any substantial or permanent employment. They were not labour-intensive and many actually displaced traditional technology and existing employment. Change was obviously needed. Out of this need was born a new conceptual approach to innovative business and technology transfer.

A workable system depends on the ability of the supplier to assemble, collate in manageable form and deliver information. This demands very full knowledge, on the supplier's part, of the quality, nature and complexity of the information to be transferred. Moreover, business concepts and technology appropriate to production, marketing and distribution, need to be made available in great variety and number. They need to be available for new business ventures and to support product-line expansion in local businesses, as well as improving existing products.

Sometimes the difference between a successful entrepreneur and a marginal or unsuccessful one is his or her ability to access information on technology, products and services. Replicable business plans, technology transfer and information services were correctly seen as being of immense help to local entrepreneurs and existing firms. Researching the basic information provided the first challenge before a workable system could be developed.

The promoters of technology centres and community programmes in the US recognised that one potential source of such technology lay in established industry. Virtually every large firm has unused or under-used technology. For a decade or more before recession most large companies had considered proposals for innovative products or services which were shelved either because they were thought to be ahead of their time or because they failed to fit the established criteria of a business plan then in place. Remarkably, once turned down or postponed for any reason, the proposal rarely resurfaced. Yet a considerable number were suitable for licencing or sale.

Another source of innovation and technology for new enterprise was found in the research programmes in academic institutions. To encourage making technology in business, universities and research laboratories available to entrepreneurs and small businesses under enterprise programmes, market research with a difference was undertaken. Under the title "Quest for Technology", this involved systematic searches for dormant technologies in industry and academic institutions. Spread over five separate states, one search alone yielded almost two hundred technologies of a very worthwhile nature. These were subsequently made available to entrepreneurs for new business start-ups.

In other researches, it was found that the basic concept for a business or a new technology had already been developed by the entrepreneur, but that he or she required the benefit of more advanced technical skills and know-how to transform the conceptual into the practical; specialist innovation support was therefore made available through the technology development programme. Another source for the Quest programme centred on the replication of businesses already in existence elsewhere. Usually, these had passed the high-risk, early start-up position and were on the second or third stages of venture capital funding. Owners of copyright and patent were persuaded to go for new markets through licensing, joint ventures or fully controlled new location plants. This brought about a substantial flow of technology across state lines.

Finally, negotiations followed for the acquisition of licences and know-how from proprietary companies or individuals. This included documentation, application data, market intelligence expertise and follow-up services. At this stage, the seed and venture capital resources of the technology centre programme played a major role in setting up local production facilities or joint ventures.

Central to the choice of using a particular technology or innovation in technology centres or community programmes was the information built up from local human resources surveys. These surveys identified the skills available for employment, or the probable success of specific training programmes to meet the need of a business planned to be established. In virtually all of the US programmes each aspect, from resources development and provision, through technology search to capital funding and identifying human resources, was seen and treated as a necessary part of the whole picture. The early success achieved by this planning caused the concept to be adopted by hundreds of other groups in different regions and states.

How can this experience and the success achieved be replicated in Ireland? Firstly, let us recognise that in population and size the whole island of Ireland is a microcosm of most states in North America. Here, as in the USA, permanent and rewarding jobs will only be created by putting together good ideas, trained people, and adequate capital to produce wealth by producing goods or services which are in demand and will be bought. Successful big business succeeds because it has the means to select these ideas, and put together the skills and capital to manufacture and market them using the most modern management tools and services. Usually, new small businesses fail, or fail to grow, because they are deficient in one or more of these areas. But if this combination is in existence – and in community enterprise sophisticated management tools and services can be shared by providing central development and resource centres – then any business however small will succeed, grow and enhance job creation.

It is accepted wisdom in Ireland that most businesses cannot show successful growth and profit unless they export: our population base is too small. On this basis it is argued that only firms of a particular size can hope to succeed and small firms lack the resources to compete in the big export market. But this analysis is only partially true, as is evidenced by some excellent work done by Bord Trachtala in organising joint promotions on behalf of small eight to fifteen-person businesses who co-operated to help find niche markets abroad. There is also the evidence, from the US example, of the extensive inter-state trading done by small fifteen to twenty-person private firms. These smaller firms usually aim for and require only a very small percentage of the total market in order to establish their success, while innovative packaging and co-operative marketing and sales arrangements can very often enhance their results. By taking on and developing new ideas through venture transfer, Irish companies can expand into new markets.

The principal barrier to the development of sufficient employment opportunities is the combined lack of investment and of appropriate business ideas. The provision of adequate investment is essentially a matter which can be solved by government action and the provision of targeted tax exemptions and benefits to investors in job creation programmes. Business ideas can come from many sources, one of which is to access them via venture and technology databasing. On the basis of the US experience of innovative venture and technology transfer from state to state, transfer here to Ireland presents no insuperable problems. The distance from east to west coast in the US is no shorter than the distance from mainland North America to this island. Of course, there is a cost, and investment will be required to achieve results without that investment showing direct high returns on capital. However, the saving in welfare costs which the resultant job creation ensures, makes government funding or specific tax concessions to investors very worthwhile.

The Physical Infrastructure

The community enterprise centre is the powerhouse of local development, and requires careful thought and assessment at the planning stage. Essentially, the centre offers small firms a place to work in an environment that is custom-built to cater for their needs. Each centre houses independent small firms, engaged in both manufacturing and services, who form a working community. By co-operating with one another they enjoy a scale of premises and facilities normally only available to larger companies. This is achieved by the use of joint service facilities, while retaining the intimate relationships and job satisfaction which come from working in a small firm.

It is in the area of physical infrastructure that communities or groups of communities can, even on their own account, play a substantial and meaningful role. Again though, these community efforts will require the type of partnership previously discussed. In addition, the task of developing this kind of infrastructure would be greatly facilitated if government acted by providing tax and other reliefs to developers or by releasing unused IDA factories for this purpose.

There is no ideal type of building. In my experience, a very wide variety of facilities have worked well as enterprise centres; these ranged from old stables and abandoned warehouses and factories to expensive purpose-built units or clusters. The simpler and cheaper the building the better, provided of course that it is consistent with the facilities which will be required. While experience suggests that optimum economy of scale is achieved at 40,000 square feet, I have seen successful units as small as 5,000 and as large as 250,000 square feet. Size is really determined by a number of factors: the premises that are available, the cost of acquiring and converting them into enterprise centres, and local conditions and population. The main criterion must be that each centre should show at least a small profit after having provided all necessary service.

Community enterprise centres are most successful when they are born from local initiative. In both the USA and parts of the UK there is a reluctance to support centres unless there has been strong local initiative in organising and financing them. Local communities must ensure that they are thoroughly involved in establishing the centre. The community's work includes providing the minimum level of local funding, premises and land which will attract support from outside agencies. There needs also to be local support for entrepreneurs by way of private funding, purchase of goods and service and finding suitable employees. At the same time the facilities must be seen to be an integral part of the community, and this is often achieved by using them for wider general community needs.

Experience also illustrates that centres established without strong direct links to funding, management and consultancy back-up score minimal success. Any one centre's potential is also enhanced when it is linked into a national or indeed international network of community enterprise centres. This is understandable when you remember that the key objective of the enterprise centre is to provide small business with access to a variety of facilities and services which they would have difficulty in locating or affording on their own. Facilities provided in the centres must be planned for both the short and long term, and must take into account every aspect of a firm's growth from the incubator stage to the optimum level of activity. Within each centre a mutually supportive community must be created amongst tenant businesspeople. To a very limited extent this happens when tenants sell their product or services within the building. More common, and more important, is the feeling of brotherhood and sisterhood in adventure, adversity and success.

The first essential task in planning a community enterprise centre is to explore the role which a centre can play in the locality. There is no universal panacea: the concept must be moulded to local situations and needs. The strategy and implementation of each support service and each enterprise situation requires local planning. This is essential if the advantage to the enterprise community is to be matched with the broader spin-off benefits to the surrounding local community. Planning requires investigation into local sociological and economic questions. This is best undertaken with professional support.

Such a study sets out to define clearly the objectives which are of mutual benefit to the centre and the local community. It would also determine the choice of tenant from an optimum location viewpoint. The study must make an accurate assessment of the community area's ability to support the growth and relocation of industry and business developed in the centre, and to forecast the employment growth potential and local housing needs. The study also needs to address the potential for friction with local businesses in the planning and provision of support service and other like factors which only properly structured research can measure.

The choice and planning of a centre requires attention to the following factors:

* Provision of a single unit, at the most central location, to house support service. The precise determination of the support service will decide the unit's size.

* An incubator unit is required to house, with maximum flexibility, the entrepreneur or inventor. These require space to develop their concepts to the point where they are ready for more substantial housing. This is the nursery for seed businesses and the laboratory from which enterprises of the future will grow. The maximum possible allocation, consistent with good economics, must be contemplated. Whether designed open-plan or in self-contained units is a matter for subjective judgement. There will always be a need for separate housing and insulation for those businesses which generate noise or dust.

* The next requirement is for separate large, independent space to accommodate more developed businesses with a higher number of in-house employees.

* In the choice of location of centres, provision must be made for the rapid expansion at a future date of businesses which are at an early stage at present. The failure of earlier centres to allow for this growth caused the more successful businesses to move out of the centre once they had grown; generally they relocated some distance away and very often in a new area. This had a direct effect on the centre because of the diminished use of facilities; there was a loss to the community in terms of jobs, but the community also lost the inspiration and example which such success provided.

Because the centre must try to suit the needs of several different kinds of business, and allow space for each of them to develop, there are critical balances to be achieved at all stages of planning. The choice of tenant determines the level of support services; that level needs to provide maximum possible growth potential to tenants. Tenant choice influences whether a balanced, integrated community is established; the community must develop as a suitable recipient for technology transfer from similar communities in the other centres. Professional assistance, working jointly with a local community, helps to avoid costly mistakes and provides a solid foundation for growth.

Having considered the community's potential to attract businesses to the centre and to develop new business ideas within it, the community enterprise group must then look for suitable local premises. Care is needed since the cost of acquiring and conversion must ultimately be reflected in rental charges. In the UK local and development authorities have made available suitable vacant premises under their ownership at little or no cost to communities. When premises are converted, it is possible to let areas from 100 square feet and upwards at minimum affordable rents which include the cost of provision (but not necessarily use) of heat, light, security and partitioning. There must be easily available access to telephone, fax, mail, office, secretarial, photocopying, interview/conference, financial, computer, consultancy, maintenance and building management services. Ideally, these are provided in-house and, very often, by entrepreneurs as separate businesses.

The community spirit is best fostered by the provision of canteen and trade library facilities where tenants can meet. Both of these facilities provide entrepreneurial opportunities for the local community. I have seen some very successful instances where community leisure facilities, such as bowling alleys, snooker halls, badminton and indoor tennis have been set up in community enterprise centres on a profit basis, and these have helped to cement community involvement.

Supporting Enterprise

IT IS PERHAPS worth looking at the experience of programmes designed to support enterprise development in Britain and in the USA, where the concept of the modern enterprise community originated.

In the 1993 budget debate in the House of Commons, it was revealed that some 250 small businesses collapsed every day in the UK, accounting for 1.75 million people on the dole. These figures startled many. Why was there such a high rate of failure? There is no simple answer. A breakdown of the small business failures shows that a very high number were involved in supplying services, and located in areas which were heavily dependent on the spending generated by a few large industries. Whether supplying directly to that industry or reliant on the purchasing power of its employees, these businesses were, like the area as a whole, tied to the success or failure of the major firm. This policy was encouraged by many of the UK agencies who concentrated on promoting the development of small businesses as suppliers, so that their existence depended, in effect, on the health of their customer.

United Kingdom governments were, certainly from the early '70s onwards, politically committed to small business development. Support service for small business was vested in state-operated development agencies, and a network of small firms centres funded by the Department of Industry provided information and counselling services. Many of the people recruited to these centres had excellent track records in the management of small or medium-sized businesses themselves and, while there was some criticism, overall the advisory service did an excellent job within the constraints of its budget. However, there was some reluctance on the part of entrepreneurs to discuss confidential business matters with a government agency.

Local authorities which established small business support programmes had a direct financial and administrative involvement in their operation. This ought to have had the effect of injecting a greater understanding of local need, but in my research and experience I found very little evidence that this was the case, except in a limited number of areas. Part of the problem was the multiplicity of agencies created, with the inherent duplication of effort and work which this implied. And indeed, by the early 1980s considerable cynicism had grown in official circles as to the programmes' effectiveness. Evidence of return in terms of jobs created or business established was poor from what had been a fairly massive investment in money, manpower and time. Aid packages for development regions and intense competition between agencies had encouraged unjustified gambles, and industries had often been badly located and as a result proved uneconomic in terms of raw material procurement and delivery to market. Some observers felt that the programme needed critical re-examination. These criticisms came from people genuinely working for and dedicated to creating a better business environment and promoting realistic job creation.

Fears were voiced of too many small businesses being assisted in a way that created major dependence on one or more large industry. There was a lack of tangible targeting of the genuine native entrepreneur and small business. Above all, there was a widespread feeling that the majority of agencies had lost sight of their key objective, to create sustainable jobs through small business development. They failed to nurture the entrepreneurial spirit and inventiveness which had originally put the UK in the forefront of the industrialised nations.

The Bolton Report on small firms published in 1971 estimated that the UK had 1.25 million small businesses. The report identified the lack of financial discipline in this sector as its major problem and put the blame squarely on the shoulders of the clearing banks. Barclays Bank responded by setting up a business advisory service. They took managers and assistant managers out of the banking system and gave them a rigorous three months training in management accounting principles. Working on the assumption that most small business management had technical rather than financial knowledge, and were thus unable or unwilling to devote sufficient time to financial management functions, Barclay's counsellors provided a free financial advice service to its small business clients. Clearly, this form of service had advantages for both bank and customer. It gave the bank a better understanding of the small business sector and its essential role in the economy, and gave small businesses access to expertise they might not otherwise have been able to afford.

However, when I discussed the programme with officers of the UK Small Business Association, some understandable reservations emerged. The conflict between the role of banker as lender and its new role as business advisor created a dilemma, both for the bank and the business person. The new service had not changed the bank's requirements for personal guarantees and collateral, and the service concentrated solely on firms' financial problems without probing in detail the factors which may have been causing these problems in the first place. Raw material procurement and marketing, for example, were seen by some business persons as more formidable hurdles than the lack of financial management skills. On the other hand, the lack of raw business experience amongst the bank's advisory staff, trained in the protected, rarefied atmosphere of banking, limited the counsellors' abilities to understand the total needs of the small businessperson or entrepreneur.

By 1978 the number of small businesses in the UK had dropped from the 1.25 million figure quoted by Bolton, to below the one million mark, though the small business sector still accounted for 20% of Gross National Product and 25% of employment. This decline prompted some banks and industrial firms to launch the London Enterprise Agency; its objective was to promote the small business sector, contribute to inner-city regeneration and act as a focal point for large firms' assistance to small business. Similar agencies were developed in about ten other cities. The agencies concentrated on giving advice, counselling and training and in some cases provided premises.

Despite the high-profile publicity which they generated, in practice the agencies suffered from limited resources. Less than one sixth of genuine enquiries were able to receive any significant measure of support. Notwithstanding this, in London alone some forty new small business start-ups, generating over 200 jobs, came about in the first twelve months operation. These were largely service industries and included such diverse enterprises as wastepaper re-cycling, furniture-making, wine bars, an engineering drafting service, a small publishing firm, theatre lighting provision, dry transfer printing, computer software, micro-electronics, screen-printing, office equipment, wine importing and plastics. Provision of help to small businesses also produced some solid results. Some 150 jobs were created by helping twenty companies expand; 400 jobs were saved and 500 created by giving targeted assistance to companies seeking to regain or expand markets. The lobbying strength of the major sponsors influenced the provision of tax incentives for workshop and enterprise unit construction. While there was a strong element of public relations promotion on the part of the large sponsoring firms, there was also evidence of a common-sense approach being taken by counsellors and of sensitivity to the interests of small business. There was, moreover, a public recognition by sponsoring finance groups that small business in the UK had made and could make a substantial contribution in terms of wealth and job creation.

It is a regrettable fact that far too much of the thrust of small business support in the UK became the private preserve of the state agencies. However, this is not the complete picture. There was a large number of projects where genuine partnership was established, where communities, local government and state agencies worked closely together to establish success. This was particularly evident in some excellent London programmes and in sponsored developments in a large number of new towns. There is also evidence, particularly since recession, of the growth of working communities in which groups of independent small firms co-operate in sharing premises and services. Many of these initiatives were born out of frustration at the inability of individuals to influence change and the state's inadequacy in meeting peoples' aspirations.

Why has the UK been so slow to recognise that its small business sector is suffering from years of neglect, and that its decline is a major contributing factor to job losses? Surely for over twenty years, the stated policy has been to help small business to grow?

Politicians may legislate for things to be done but the power to implement policies is vested in the civil service, the local authority and/or the semi-state agencies. If they misunderstand, or subjectively interpret the ordinance they are given, the results can be far removed from those intended. In the UK, as in Ireland, the role of the state as grand provider is sacred to politicians and administrators alike. In the UK this doctrine has been coupled with the "two nations" policies of the Conservative government for more than twelve years. The divisions wrought by anti-trade union legislation, the coal mining dispute, the guerrilla warfare generated by the poll tax and the combative stance between central and local government creates a climate which militates against the success of any small business programme.

In the UK there also exists in the corridors of power a flawed belief that recession is the only and principal cause of unemployment, and it is wrongly assumed that an upturn in the world economic situation will largely solve the problem. This thinking ignores the massive changes in technology which have altered production methods so dramatically, and successive governments have consistently failed to give adequate financial incentives for the very substantial investment required if industry is to adapt; indeed in many respects investment has been penalised. Until these factors are addressed the UK will be left with a hard core of unemployment and the problem will be particularly intense in the inner city areas. Finally, none of the UK programmes were as professionally designed or managed as their US counterparts. They lacked some of the key elements which, as I will later outline, are required for success, and there was an almost total non-recognition of the need for innovation and technology transfer.

It is probably not difficult to understand why the authorities in Britain and Ireland were reluctant to promote programmes like those found in the USA. There appears to be a deep-rooted distaste for genuine community empowerment in both countries. It is true that the Irish and UK state agencies did copy some aspects of the US programmes, but they either failed to understand or refused to accept the real innovative thinking involved. As a result they ended up, in most cases, building glorified workshops rather than true resource centres, and failure rates were exceptionally high. Part of the reason is that virtually all of these agencies insisted on state ownership and control of the centres.

In a survey of these centres, Wiesner and Hoffman of the Massachussets Institute of Technology reported:

These institutes... are not doing well because they are bureaucratically oriented government institutions that could neither attract nor hold a real entrepreneur... typically a guy who likes to take shortcuts, doesn't believe in paperwork, carries all his ideas in his head, wants to make his own decisions ... he couldn't survive two weeks in state controlled centres.

Some years ago the former National Enterprise Agency reported a failure rate of over 90% in Irish state programmes and advised that future development should more closely imitate the US model. However, both politicians and senior state planners continue to insist on a highly centralised form of administration. The very rigid control which the Department of Finance exercises over all European Community funding is but one example of this attitude in practice. There is a deep reluctance to support genuine community development and, despite the lip-service, a fear of community empowerment. The powers of our local authorities, too, have been stripped to an unacceptable level – a step which even Mrs Thatcher's government lacked the courage to adopt.

The first step to a solution of our present critical unemployment problems is to admit that the massive centralising of power has been a failure. It has brought "Ireland Inc." to near insolvency. Government needs to re-define its role and manage its operations in new ways. We require the adoption of a more entrepreneurial approach that anticipates needs, identifies priorities and opportunities, and encourages an effective coalition of public, community and private efforts. It is instructive to look at how this small-business led development has been supported in the USA.

In 1981 I had the task of reviewing and reporting on the support services for small businesses operated by governmental agencies, public bodies and private charities in the USA. The study covered over fifty separate locations in seven different states.

Federal statistics showed that 87% of all new jobs created in the USA in the eleven years 1969-79 were created by small business, 50% of new product ideas came from the small business category and 45% of GNP was attributable to small business operations. To avoid any misunderstanding, I questioned the federal authority on their definition of small business, and was informed that the majority in the reports were in the five to thirty-five employee bracket.

A Small Business Council set up by the Governor of Pennsylvania reported in May 1980:

Small business is the sector of this state's economy accounting for the majority of new jobs, thus with the best potential for new job development ...

With this recognition comes the opportunity to pioneer and develop systems and models with the potential to point the way for small business not only here [in Pennsylvania] but all across the nation.

However, the first, rather startling finding of my study was that small business appeared to have developed despite, rather than because of, state support systems. It was obvious that in the first decade of the federal Small Business Administration programme, established in the early 1970s, progress had been hampered by official prejudice and scepticism as to whether the time and resources required to support small businesses would be justified in terms of job creation. This prejudice was compounded by the fact that schools of economics and business studies in most of the larger universities, which derived substantial support from big business, gave little time to studying the importance and the economics of small-scale enterprise. Eventually the federal government did come to recognise the importance of small business and the strategic value of a small business support programme, but because the US government had set up the SBA as a federal agency, individual states did not take complementary measures to implement its work locally. Moreover, the government confined itself to setting out the objectives for which funds were to be allocated; the implementation of these objectives depended on matching action at state level. There was confusion at local level as to how to cater for the needs of small business, and federal funds quickly became absorbed in supporting a vast, multi-tiered bureaucracy. In one state alone there were six separate agencies administering these funds.

The principal exceptions to this waste were two volunteer programmes organised by the federal authorities under the Small Business Administration – the Service Corps of Retired Executives (SCORE) and the Active Corps of Executives (ACE). Established in 1964, SCORE provided 8,000 professionally qualified and experienced counsellors in over 330 locations spread over fifty states and Puerto Rico, then a United States protectorate. ACE, established in 1969, was a working partner with SCORE. Its members, still active in business, furnished special talents not represented by SCORE in any specific location. Volunteers from these agencies worked in their own communities or nearby, providing services to businesses which qualified under the SBA programme. All expenses incurred were re-imbursed by the SBA. These counsellors achieved an excellent track record in assisting small business development, and many were subsequently recruited to the International Executive Service Corps, a wide-ranging consultancy service to third world countries which is offered as part of United States foreign aid.

Operating at federal level the Small Business Administration acted as a guarantor for borrowers and gave direct loans in a variety of situations to small businesses, local developments, minority enterprise and small business investment groups. This was a substantial help in developing business and technology centres and community enterprise programmes. In Massachusetts the federal programme was coupled effectively with local state funding, and contributed to very significant employment growth in high-technology developments such as the manufacture of computer equipment, measure and control instruments, optical instruments and lenses and certain types of diagnostic aids for the medical sector. Even during recession these areas continued to show employment growth rates of between 13% and 33%.

But the "small is beautiful" campaign did not get into gear just because of federal or state action. It came from a recognition in the mid-'70s, principally in the technology and engineering schools, that economic development, job opportunity and innovative growth needed assistance. These institutions provided direct, practical business consultancy to inventors and to entrepreneurs in new and planned commercial ventures. They helped ordinary citizens develop successful enterprises from their own ideas, products and innovations.

Studies conducted by the Applied Research Centre, Wharton School at the University of Pennsylvania, the Federal University Development Corporation and the Massachusetts Institute of

Technology, led to the inescapable conclusion that:

* Economic development and stability of employment were best achieved by giving major support to small businesses.

* Small business was in general more resistant than big business to the cold winds of recession.

* From a sociological viewpoint, communities were generally better served by small business than by the establishment and reliance on a single major industry.

As the movement to support small-scale industry gathered ground, industrial resource development programmes were set up by more than thirty third-level institutes in over eight states to serve the dual role of providing job experience to graduates and undergraduates whilst simultaneously giving free business consultancy to investors and entrepreneurs. Detailed business plans were drawn up for businesses just getting off the ground, or ideas and new products were referred to potential investors. MIT provided laboratory facilities for the development and testing of new products and offered entrepreneurs a professional engineering support service. The Inventors Association of New England organised a lecture and seminar programme for small businesses pursuing the development of new inventions.

The most ambitious programme was undertaken by a network of university and college centres headed by the Wharton School at the University of Pennsylvania and supported by all of that state's universities. These centres received 50% of their funding from federal sources; the balance came from the state, the universities and local private sources. The funding formula permitted the maximum leverage and targeting of federal funds and it enabled the programme to offer state-wide service to local business people. Resources were largely used to counsel and train newly established small businesses in areas such as accounting, advertising, marketing, government procurement, personnel management and bank relations. The programme also provided start-up assistance in making financial projections and loan applications and offered a network of sophisticated technical and management consultancy services. It was directed at the small business community as a whole, though there was also a special emphasis on minority owned businesses, women entrepreneurs and new business start-ups. The programme provided one-to-one counselling and consultancy to over 3,500 small businesses each year. This was clear recognition of the value of small business to the state; it emphasised that the growth of these businesses was vital to the economy of both the state and the nation.

Why then did it take a recession to demonstrate so clearly, on a national basis, the importance of small business in terms of employment and economic stability? One Harvard graduate, heading up one of the programmes, summarised what I found to be a majority viewpoint: "Up to recession we thought Harvard had all the answers, and Harvard thought the answers lay in big business!"

The community-level business centre/enterprise centre development was described by one contemporary commentator as "the new industrial revolution". It demonstrated also that a very large number of people found greater job satisfaction working in smaller units than in corporate structures. Central to the whole US experience was the fact that government funding was most productive and cost-effective when put into well planned, supervised programmes, sponsored by business or by the community. The funding was targeted to creating and maintaining actual businesses operating profitably and providing worthwhile employment; it was not used for make-work programmes or spent on training for non-existent jobs. It is, however, well to remember that without the support of government funding, business and community projects could not have achieved the same results on their own. This was shown when federal funding support was severely curtailed under successive Republican administrations.

At the end of my review of US developments I was driven to the inescapable conclusion that, despite some area of waste, the federal programme had unleashed a new era of positive development of small business. One of the unusual features of some of the most successfull programmes in the USA was that, unlike their Irish and UK counterparts, they saw no reason to provide statistics on job creation or job preservation in their annual reports or promotional literature. When I queried this practice, the director of several of these programmes indicated that they saw no need to divert scarce resources to obtaining, analysing and publishing such information. Nonetheless, even the harshest critics of the federal programmes and the agencies readily admitted that their job creation and job preservation achievements were substantial by any criteria. SCORE for example, could justifiably claim that its results in terms of jobs created or preserved ran into millions; the agency's critics, while arguing that these figures masked the uneven quality of SCORE's service throughout the USA and its failure to provide any service in some areas, accepted these job creation estimates as valid.

The lack of adequate statistics did create a major drawback in that state and federal legislators were not alerted to the vital importance of small business as soon as they might have been. It was only after research was commissioned that the national importance of small business in the creation of new jobs and, the development of new products and the contribution of small business to GNP, came to be realised. Research in Pennsylvania, for example, showed that small business accounted for the majority of new job creation and had the best potential for further job growth. The Small Business Development centres in that state were credited by independent observers with preserving over 250,000 jobs in companies at risk through the provision of consulting services. The director of the programme guess-estimated job creation at 25,000 in the first two years of the programme.

Many of the business and technology centres which were encouraged to set up by the availability of 59% federal funding created upwards of 600 new jobs each year for the first five years of their operation. Indirect employment arising from ideas developed in these centres, which became the basis of starting or expanding small businesses, substantially increased these figures. Most of the centres merged support service for small industry with the community, and the results were impressive not only as regards job creation, but also from the point of view of good human relations, which led in time to good labour relations. The very low rate of failure of businesses which started life in these centres was equally impressive, and continued after the business left the centre in order to expand.

Statistics do not, of course, tell the full story. More importantly, at a time when business in general was cursing the darkness of recession, bright candles were being lit by programmes such as these. They received considerable exposure through local and national media, partly because the programmes themselves were seen as new and innovative, partly because new, inventive ideas and technologies were being developed in the technology centres. The effect of these centres on the wider local community was also seen to be dramatic. Local residents, whether directly involved or not, felt a sense of pride in the progress being achieved in their community.

Turning the Tide

OVER FORTY YEARS ago, economics journalist Arnold Marsh wrote in the *Irish Review* that there could be no neutrals in the fight against poverty, unemployment, discontent and emigration. Developing his thesis on job creation, Marsh argued that there was an urgent need for more co-operative development along the lines of the Finnish and Scandinavian models. He saw the local co-operative society as "a centre of help, education, and social and business life", a definition which might equally be applied to the modern community enterprise initiative.

Marsh argued that the state should give a lead in developing Irish resources, and the list of areas which he pinpointed makes fascinating reading today. He called for a programme of afforestation, the conversion of sewage into fertiliser and methane gas, and the provision of hatcheries for fresh-water fisheries development. He wanted to utilise wind-energy, either to pump water to high-level reservoirs for the general supply of electricity, or for the production by electrolysis of hydrogen as a source of motive power. He pointed to the resources which we might cull from the sea by extracting minerals like magnesium, copper, iodine and bromine from seaweed, and called for the exploration and development of our land-based mineral resources and the use of turf as a raw material for the chemical industry. To grow warm-climate and out-of-season fruit and vegetables he urged that the use of glasshouse growing should be greatly extended. And, pointing to the need to conserve resources, he insisted we should regulate water levels instead of draining land haphazardly by gravity alone, and increase the storage capacity of the Shannon system by means of embankment and pumping. He also pointed out that if we were to make the best use of the resources we enjoyed, we needed to encourage research and development programmes, particularly in our third-level institutions.

Marsh argued against building up industries to compete on the world stage except where we had a special advantage, since "depending on them would only make us helpless in times of general trade depression". A better plan, he suggested, was to secure and maintain a bigger market at home. He called on government to introduce tax relief on profits which were re-invested in business and to provide capital loans at attractive terms to encourage the native entrepreneur. As for the state,

> it could, and should, embark on enterprises that would bring prosperity to the nation, even though they might not at first have any prospects of making direct profits. It should do so on a large enough scale to take up whatever slack may exist in employment. The list of promising projects of this kind is long but embarking on them on as large a scale as is feasible will bring prosperity and contentment at once, together with a great increase in our national resources.

Marsh admitted that a programme of this nature would cost over £500 million to introduce but argued that we could not wage a successful war against unemployment and emigration "if we demand direct dividends from every item of national investment".

Marsh was writing at a time when the concept of self-sufficiency was still alive, and more than ten years before the First Programme for Economic Expansion. There is little evidence that his words were taken seriously. The late Dr David Thornley, Associate Professor of Political Science at Trinity College, reflected the more widely-held view of Irish economic potential in his introduction to Basil Chubb's study in 1970:

> Two basic factors, one economic and one geographic, have for long cast their shadow over the politics of Ireland. The first is that the island posesses no abundance of mineral re-

sources and, consequently, no tradition of industrial development. This means that Ireland has been dependent for its national wealth upon agricultural production, and upon importation for the bulk of the artifacts that sustain industrial civilisation. Today and for the foreseeable future, Ireland is, therefore, defined by economic circumstances as essentially an exporter of primary agricultural produce, notably cattle, and an importer of heavy industrial equipment and consumer goods. For these reasons the Irish people have for centuries been condemned to the proportionately low standard of living that is often the concomitant of agricultural production; it has also made Irish economics, and therefore Irish politics, abnormally sensitive to external forces over which the political state of Ireland can have no control.[1]

This description mirrors the view of Ireland which was held by administrators prior to independence, and adopted, seemingly without question, by successive governments since then. It is my conviction that this vision, if vision it can be called, is based on an assessment which was and is largely untested. If we had carried out an open-minded analysis of the strengths and weaknesses of the nation, we would have discovered the potential of our resources; this potential provides the only sound basis on which to develop the economy. This work has been carried out to some extent in the exploitation of natural gas, lead and zinc, but at best it is undertaken only in a piecemeal fashion. Even today, the potential of the seas around us remains a mystery. A representative of the Irish Geological Survey Office remarks: "90% of what we now know about the seabed around our coast has been learned in the past twenty-five to thirty years. What we don't know would still fill volumes." Rather than look at our resources and plan their development, our entire economic planning seems to be predicated on how best we can maximise grants from the European Community. Yet, as economist Raymond Crotty points out in a review of our EC membership, looking to Europe can be no answer to the problems which persist at home.

It cannot be claimed that the present disasters of massive, intractable unemployment, extreme dependence on foreign trade, and a currency undermined by State debt and bereft of the defence of exchange controls, were unforseeable. They were predictable, in broad outline if not in detail, as the inevitable consequence of joining the EC and tying Ireland's economy, with its long-standing structural weaknesses, to the common policies of a Community comprising countries with circumstances entirely different from Ireland's.

EC membership secured "markets in Europe" for Ireland's expanded exports; but not "jobs at home" for the people. The growth of those exports reflected the willingness of governments to subsidise them with borrowed funds, not the economy's efficiency. The latter was more accurately reflected by the virtual obliteration of indigenous industry producing for the home market and by the consequent growth of imports. These grew almost *pari passu* with exports.

State debt, incurred in the first instance to give subsidies and tax holidays to exporters and subsequently to cover interest charges on existing debt, increased in line with both exports and imports. Unemployment tracked both the growth of foreign trade – or rather imports – and the growth of State debt – or rather the cost of servicing it. Unemployment is now four to five times greater than when Ireland joined the EC.

It is time for the nation to reject the dependence on the EC which, over the past 20 and more years, has led to the present impasse. It is time to learn from those other small west European nations – Iceland, Norway, Sweden, Finland, Austria and Switzerland – which, from a base at or below the Irish level 70 years ago, have since, by an effective exercise of sovereignty to pursue policies appropriate to their circumstances, secured incomes that are now twice or three times higher than those in Ireland; have zero emigration; and have unemployment which is about one-tenth of the Irish level. It is time now for change.[2]

This culture of dependency which lies at the heart of our present economic difficulty is the primary problem we must confront. I do not believe that we have been ruled since independence by knaves or fools. However, I do contend that we inherited and held on to a system of government which produced a cumbersome and costly administration. Kevin O'Higgins, Minister for Home Affairs in the first Irish government, was perhaps searching for a more efficient system when he called for a parliament of independent deputies, which would be responsible for enacting legislation, and a Cabinet which would work with extern ministers chosen for their administrative expertise, elected individually by the Dáil and directly and individually responsible for their departments. His proposal was "enacted only in an emasculated form and abandoned after six years".[3]

Some seventy years later, politicians themselves are obliged to admit that people have grown disillusioned with politics, do not trust politicians and have little or no faith in any of the political parties. The leader of Fine Gael, John Bruton, acknowledges: "People have not rejected the original purposes which parliamentary institutions were set up to achieve... but they see them as unable to deliver."[4]

If people have little faith in the political process it is because they see very clearly that the priority of politicians is their own re-election, and that they tackle issues on the basis of whether or not they attract enough attention to carry votes. Politicians are prisoners of their own mythology. Many will, for example, admit privately that they see little hope of reducing unemployment if policies continue as they are, but publically they continue the charade. There are plans to bring government closer to the people by establishing regional authorities in the immediate future, though the precise detail of their function has yet to be finalised. However, it will include "co-ordination... of public services at regional level, including co-ordination of decisions on major items of expenditure on the arts (e.g. theatres)" and they will also have a role in "monitoring and advising on the implementation at regional level" of the various EC-funded programmes. But the tasks of monitoring, advising and co-ordinating do not amount to real powers, and, as Frank McDonald of *The Irish Times* points out, "the most important role which might be performed by the new regional authorities has been omitted. This is the area of strategic planning..."[5]

There is a shortfall of real representation in these new authorities, which will consist entirely of city or county councillors appointed by their own local authorities rather than directly elected by the voters. In any event, a real attempt to decentralise power would surely concern itself with devolving authority to the local government already in place, rather than forever creating more institutions. In this light, too, the new county enterprise boards, while they represent a welcome step towards recognising the need to encourage initiative from the grassroots, may in the end result in a further diffusion of local energy. It is difficult to avoid agreeing with a recent commentary which sees the regional authority proposals as expressing "the mania for central control through bureaucracy" rather than a real attempt to give people an effective say in their own affairs.[6]

This is more than unfortunate at a time when our greatest need is for a convergence between political power and community aspirations. As writer John Waters remarks:

Although the growth of community activity is now widespread, its very nature does not allow it to be perceived as a national *movement*. Networks are beginning to be forged, but this is at a preliminary stage. Most of the achievements have been localised, and thefore largely invisible. The nature of the change is therefore best perceived in philosophical terms. Community enterprise is not simply about reforming the operations of the failed centralised State, but about finding an alternative way of seeing and doing. [7]

We need more than anything to get away from the coercive jurisdiction of central government in all matters affecting our

lives, and this can only come about when communities themselves change. We must take responsibility for our own future,
not as isolated individuals but as organised communities, and
make change in the structure and policies of government a political imperative. The power of communities is demanded
nowhere more urgently than in the field of employment, and
the potential which communities have here is fully recognised.
Brendan O'Regan, the father of Ireland's most succesful regional initiative, SFADCO, is not alone when he expresses the
belief that the solution to unemployment will not come from
the state agencies, but will have to be worked out in and by
communities.

Yet there is very real evidence of the general public distanc-
ing themselves from the problems of poverty and unemployment. Despite excellent reports from Combat Poverty, the
Conference of Religious Superiors and others, there exists an
almost naive belief that if we ignore the problems, they will go
away. To this extent there is a frightening similarity between
Irish society today and that of the United States during the latter part of the 1950s, when the dollar was strong and there
was little to disturb the free-spending enjoyment of the affluent. It was good to be American, provided you were white,
free and part of the general prosperity. It was different for the
blacks and Hispanics of the ghettos, but few were concerned
about their plight. "Let the bums find work" was the constant
catchphrase. No one would concede that the seeds of social
destruction were actually in place. No one expected the explosion of hatred and savagery that erupted in the early 1960s.
When they came, the racial riots caused outrage, alarm and
disbelief.

Addressing the Catholic Social Service Conference in
September 1993, the Archbishop of Dublin, Dr Desmond
O'Connell, condemned unemployment as a scandal "that was
getting worse". Pointing out that in some areas as many as 70-
80% of adults were out of work, the Archbishop said: "the
greatest single social problem confronting society today is the

subversive level of unemployment". It is not difficult to see how high levels of unemployment can subvert the norms of social life in an environment where the unemployed feel rejected by society, where whole communities look on the political process with a level of cynicism which borders on contempt. We need to break away from this tendency to "ghettoise" the problem of the unemployed, which is really a way of pushing the problem out of our sight in the hope that we will not be contaminated by it. We must integrate the problems of the unemployed into the problems of the community as a whole.

Community enterprise initiatives can take on this task in an especially valuable way if they make counselling for the unemployed an essential part of the overall community programme; in the Tallaght programme, confidential counselling is provided to everyone who wants to avail of it. All unemployed people need support, a helping hand through the maze of problems which unemployment brings. It is sometimes intensely difficult for unemployed people to overcome the negative feelings which being out of work inevitably brings, to take on instead a courageous, positive attitude which works to make opportunities available. Counselling encourages no false optimism, but it does offer a compassionate ear to the man or woman without a job, a professional evaluation of his or her prospects, and guidance to help them work out solutions to the situation they find themselves in.

My first introduction to counselling of this kind came in the late 1970s when I was privileged to attend a seminar run by a group of counsellors who had spearheaded the effort to win back the hearts and minds of disillusioned and angry people in the aftermath of the racial riots in US cities. The credit for the social rejuvenation which the community enterprise initiatives brought to the ghettos went to the programmes' authors and sponsors, but in the view of many observers the counsellors were the unsung heroes of the battle.

In a community enterprise programme counselling will attempt to encourage the productive ability of the unemployed person, but its ambit is broader than career guidance or an assessment of the business potential of an idea for self-employment or enterprise. The counsellor must uncover the true potential of the person before her. She, or he, must be able to look behind the mask of despair or false bravado which many unemployed people take on as a result of feeling socially rejected; the counsellor must bring to light the whole person and encourage them to assess their own potential. The counsellor also needs to know when not to intervene; in some cases it is wiser to refer to other services which are more appropriate, and to assist the person who has come for counselling to make contact with them. At a time when we have training courses for virtually all forms of human activity, it is a pity that training in counselling is not widely available in Ireland. This would be an excellent programme for our third-level institutions to adopt, or indeed it could be undertaken by the provision of training in every diocese. The careful training of suitable counsellors is an essential factor in promoting a meaningful response to unemployment, not least because it deals with unemployment as a human and not solely an economic problem.

Unemployment is not dealt with by putting it at the top of a government agenda. To get to a solution we need to mobilise all our resources, most of all our human resources, and make deep-rooted changes in our social attitudes and priorities. The starting point for this departure will only come when people are brought into the decision-making process through a process of community empowerment. This will require change at all levels. Trade unions could play a valuable part if they were to widen their role to include general community problems in addition to their focus on the workplace. In a rapidly changing employment situation, the traditional workplace may not exist in quite the same way in the future; unions also need to change so as to be able to express and represent the real needs of people both in and out of work. On the other hand, the problem of unemployment is inseparable from the movement for greater democracy within industry. If a job is worth fighting for, it must be a good one. One way to make sure this is so is to give more power and involvement to the people in work.

But most of all we require a change of attitude about work and the part it plays in our lives. We have been brainwashed with the idea that monetary reward is the main criteria for determining the worth of a job – the meaning and fulfilment which work brings to our lives is given a low ranking in this scale of values. This social perspective devalues the status of those doing poorly paid work or working at home, and disregards the value of people who put productive effort into community activities. Yet self-employment – which includes work in the home – job sharing and community welfare work are all options which need to be considered at the present time, in order to encourage people to engage in a role which enables their gifts to be used in a way which will bring meaning to their own lives and the lives of others.

It is an indictment of our society that there are, for example, long waiting lists for housing at a time of high unemployment, and that social, environmental and other schemes cannot be carried out even when they are sorely needed. All too often, our precedent-dominated policies block new creative energy, and pay for it in an ever-increasing social welfare bill. The task of effecting the changes in the social welfare system to enable claimants to earn money and work their way towards either co-operative or self employment may be complex, but it is hardly insuperable. In addition, we need perhaps to accept a new category of "voluntary unemployed". This would grant a higher rate of long-term unemployment benefit to those who wished to use their time constructively for the benefit of the community, such as giving help to the disadvantaged or providing homecare, which many find more fulfilling than working in the marketplace. The depth of the crisis we face demands that we develop policies which are appropriate for the transition to a new and better way of organising our working lives. In broad terms, policy ought to be enabling, allowing and encouraging people to do what they want to do and removing unnecessary blocks to productive activity.

Social and economic rejuvenation can only come about if all sectors of society band together to tackle the social problems in their communities. Those who take this initiative demonstrate their belief and willingness to tackle the problems with the use of their own resources. The task is not easy. In the first flush of enthusiasm and uplift almost everything seems possible. Volunteers offer their service on an almost open ended basis; dedicated and experienced members of the community give advice and encouragement. A new sense of hope is created and people expect things to happen instantaneously. But change cannot and will not happen overnight; there can only be a sound prospect of renewal if the community initiative persists over time.

In pressing ahead with a community enterprise programme an immense workload is shouldered by voluntary committees and their members. They have to initiate action and follow it through. They are usually learning by experience, the slowest method of learning, and at the same time they are trying to attend to their personal lives. Is it any wonder that delays are experienced and wrong decisions are taken? The sharp edge of enthusiasm may be dulled as divisions begin to appear, targets are lowered, at worst the whole project founders. This situation can be countered if the community has available the services of an experienced consultant during the initial stages of the community enterprise programme; at a very minimum, initial seminar training by such a professional can avoid unnecessary delays, wasted effort and expense. At all events, community groups must learn the value of hastening slowly, of building on the solid foundations of a series of intermediate objectives, understanding that these apparently small steps make greater achievements possible.

Through our combined efforts we can establish the strengths

and weaknesses of our own local economies, determine what action is needed to improve our present position and create sustainable growth. Using this framework community enterprise will achieve its goals of generating employment and restoring the economic and social fabric of the society in which we live. The nationwide growth of community structures will be the catalyst which forces greater empowerment of the people through restoring real power to the locality and establishing a solid basis for genuine partnership between people and government.

While it is impossible to produce a single plan which can be applied universally to all communities, we have suggested some goals and structures to help communities to achieve their ambitions. There are doubtless many other approaches which will emerge from the work of local communities, and so there should be: community enterprise is most of all about initiative, about finding new and better ways of doing things. The key objective is to end the tragic waste of human life which is caused by unemployment, and to help build a better future for ourselves. We have nothing to fear from the future if we act to take control of our own destiny. A dream? Perhaps. But, as Pearse said to a previous generation, what if the dream be true?

Notes

1. Basil Chubb, *The Government and Politics of Ireland,* OUP, 1970, p.1
2. *Cork Examiner,* 18 August 1993
3. Chubb, op. cit. p.181
4. *The Irish Times,* 8 September 1993
5. *The Irish Times,* 2 June 1993
6. *Intercom,* July 1993, Catholic Communications Institute of Ireland
7. *The Irish Times,* 2 June 1993